Praise for
The Chutzpah Imperative:
Empowering Today's Jews for a Life That Matters

"Ed Feinstein might not have invented chutzpah, but he certainly has reclaimed it for the Jewish people. *The Chutzpah Imperative* is the perfect antidote to what is ailing us."

—**Craig Taubman**, singer-songwriter and producer;
founder, Craig 'n Co.

"Profound, elegant and beautiful.... Rabbi Ed Feinstein is able to take the great classic stories of our tradition and shed new light and wisdom on them. Whether you are just learning about Judaism or have spent your life steeped in learning Torah, Ed Feinstein will give you new things to think about, transforming old understandings into brilliant, fresh approaches. Compelling, humorous and instructive ... hooray for Rabbi Feinstein's chutzpah in this breakthrough book that every generation from every background will enjoy."

—**Rabbi Asher Lopatin**, president,
Yeshivat Chovevei Torah Rabbinical School

"With the art of a storyteller, the craft of an educator and the wisdom of a philosopher, Rabbi Ed Feinstein guides us through the epic tales of our past and shows us again and again from where a Jew's dogged perseverance and vital engagement with the world emanates. He skillfully adjusts the focus for those of us who see through a Jewish lens, and presents a compelling picture for those who are looking for one."

—**Harlene Winnick Appelman**, executive director,
Covenant Foundation

"It's extraordinary how Rabbi Ed Feinstein has managed to place the aggressive and seemingly secular notion of 'chutzpah' at the heart of Judaism. But he's right: It will take nothing less than chutzpah for this ancient tradition to realize its potential. Feinstein needed chutzpah to bring holiness to chutzpah."

—**David Suissa**, president, Tribe Media/*Jewish Journal*

"Nudges us into an honest life, a compassionate path, questioning our way to goodness and to glory. This book will break your heart wide open, welcoming in the whole wide world."

—**Rabbi Bradley Shavit Artson, DHL**, vice president, American Jewish University; author, *God of Becoming and Relationship: The Dynamic Nature of Process Theology*

The
CHUTZPAH
Imperative

The
CHUTZPAH
Imperative

Empowering Today's Jews
for a
Life That Matters

Rabbi Edward Feinstein

Foreword by Rabbi Laura Geller

For People of All Faiths, All Backgrounds

JEWISH LIGHTS Publishing

Woodstock, Vermont

The Chutzpah Imperative: Empowering Today's Jews for a Life That Matters

2014 Hardcover Edition, First Printing

© 2014 by Edward Feinstein

Foreword © 2014 by Laura Geller

For information regarding permission to reprint material from this book, please mail or fax your request in writing to Jewish Lights Publishing, Permissions Department, at the address / fax number listed below, or e-mail your request to permissions@jewishlights.com.

Grateful acknowledgment is given for permission to use lyrics from "Don't Fence Me In," words and music by Cole Porter, copyright © 1944 (Renewed) WB Music Corp. All rights reserved. Used by permission of Alfred Music.

"Do You Love Me?," copyright © 1964 by Sheldon Harnick and Jerry Bock. Publication and Allied Rights owned by Mayerling Productions Ltd. (Administered by R&H Music) and Jerry Bock Enterprises for the United States and Alley Music Corporation, Trio Music Company, and to Jerry Bock Enterprises for the world outside of the United States. Used by permission. All rights reserved.

Library of Congress Cataloging-in-Publication Data

Feinstein, Edward, 1954–

The chutzpah imperative : empowering today's Jews for a life that matters / Rabbi Edward Feinstein ; foreword by Rabbi Laura Geller.

pages cm

Includes bibliographical references.

ISBN 978-1-58023-792-5 — ISBN 978-1-58023-815-1 (ebook) 1. Jewish way of life. 2. Judaism. I. Title.

BM723.F4298 2014

296.7—dc23

2014027022

10 9 8 7 6 5 4 3 2 1

Manufactured in the United States of America

Jacket and Interior Design: Tim Holtz

For People of All Faiths, All Backgrounds

Published by Jewish Lights Publishing

A Division of LongHill Partners, Inc.

Sunset Farm Offices, Route 4, P.O. Box 237

Woodstock, VT 05091

Tel: (802) 457-4000   Fax: (802) 457-4004

www.jewishlights.com

For my teacher, Rabbi Harold Schulweis,
who taught me to question.

CONTENTS

FOREWORD

Rabbi Laura Geller

"If there is a God," the rabbi began his invocation, "then God is like the man we honor tonight." The several thousand people in the theater suddenly got quiet. "If there is a God," the rabbi continued, "then God cares about people the way the man we honor tonight cares." "If there is a God ..."

Did I hear that correctly? Is that rabbi asking if there is a God? Can rabbis even ask that question? Is that rabbi suggesting that we can learn about God by believing that individuals can make a difference in the world?

By asking a transgressive question that rabbis never ask, this rabbi both honored an extraordinary Jewish cultural giant and in the same breath challenged his audience to think about God and what it means to be a human being. Talk about chutzpah! The one being honored was actor and composer Theodore Bikel; the rabbi was Ed Feinstein, the same Ed Feinstein who wrote *Tough Questions Jews Ask: A Young Adult's Guide to Building a Jewish Life*, a book that gives young people permission to ask questions about whether Judaism matters.

Ed Feinstein has chutzpah, the audacious courage to name the real problem of contemporary Jewish life: we don't ask enough of our Judaism. It is no longer sufficient to define Jewishness as a reaction to the Holocaust or through vicarious identification with Israel. To really matter, Jewishness needs to be more than nostalgia or ethnicity. It needs to answer the questions that he has the chutzpah to ask:

What truth lies within the Jewish experience that might bring purpose to my life?

What grand narrative at the heart of Jewish life claims me?

What is the meaning of being Jewish today?

And then he has the chutzpah to answer: human beings are God's partners in repairing the world. Human beings matter; we are not powerless. God needs us. Rabbi Feinstein calls this "the chutzpah imperative."

What makes this book so extraordinary is that Rabbi Feinstein takes us on a journey through the Jewish story to show us how this chutzpah evolves, beginning with the biblical narratives and leading us masterfully through the unfolding of Jewish commentary, theology, and philosophy, and through changing notions of Divinity. The book is one of the best and most thoughtful introductions to the major ideas and thinkers of Judaism through the ages—and so much more. It is also a challenge to engage with Jewish tradition in order to imagine the horizons of human possibility.

Rabbi Feinstein has had extraordinary teachers. Among them were Rabbi Harold Schulweis, to whom the book is dedicated, and Rabbi David Hartman (z"l), who created the Shalom Hartman Institute in Jerusalem. Each of them might be among those whom the Talmud describes as showing "chutzpah even in the face of heaven." Each has been willing to demand justice, to appeal for compassion, to speak truth to power. Rabbi Feinstein stands on their shoulders. With this book as our guide, we can stand on his.

We might not yet ask that of our Judaism but this is what it asks of us.

ACKNOWLEDGMENTS

Chutzpah is not born of its own. Chutzpah may shine in an exceptional individual, but in reality, it is a collective project. Chutzpah is nurtured by a culture, sustained by a community, and shared through generations. And so, too, any book that celebrates chutzpah.

I am indebted to the teachers who inspired my chutzpah, Rabbi Irving "Yitz" Greenberg, Rabbi David Hartman (*z"l*), and my mentor, Rabbi Harold Schulweis. I am grateful to the communities of learning that encourage my chutzpah, most especially Valley Beth Shalom, the Ziegler Rabbinical School of American Jewish University, the Wexner Heritage Program, and the Shalom Hartman Institute. I am grateful for twenty years of learning and inspiration with my *chevruta*-in-chutzpah, Rabbi Mark Borovitz. I was blessed to grow up in a home that taught chutzpah. I am thankful for my parents Dov and Chaiky (*z"l*) Feinstein, and Herb and Geri Bieber, and for my brothers, Larry, Simmy, and Jerry. And I am humbled to have received gifts that no amount of chutzpah could have asked for, a loving soul mate, Nina, and our children, Yonah, Nessa, and Raffi.

My deepest appreciation to Emily Wichland, vice president of Editorial and Production at Jewish Lights, for her encouragement, editorial brilliance, and endless kindness. And to Stuart M. Matlins, founder and publisher of Jewish Lights, who has provided a voice for our generation's spiritual creativity, moral yearning, and prayers of hope. May God only add to your chutzpah!

Introduction

THE WICKED CHILD'S QUESTION

We don't ask enough of our Judaism.

We American Jews are proud to be Jewish. But for most, we prize being Jewish only for the aesthetic appeal, the ethnic charm. We cherish the endearing Yiddish phrases, bagels and lox on Sunday mornings, family moments at the Pesach Seder, exchanging presents on Hanukkah, the rituals of holidays that echo traditions of generations gone by. This is a Judaism of warm, ethnic sentimentality that demands very little of us and in return offers little spiritual wisdom.

We American Jews are proud of our heritage, our people, and Israel. Pride, belonging, custom, we have. But Jewishness has little influence on the lives most American Jews live. Being Jewish doesn't really shape our choices, our ethics, the way we understand life.

We don't ask enough of our Judaism because we rarely get beyond the superficial ethnic decoration. We haven't asked: What truth lies within the Jewish experience that might bring purpose to my life? What grand narrative at the heart of Jewish life claims me? What is the meaning of being Jewish today?

We haven't asked because we've been taught not to ask.

We have just witnessed the most traumatic century in all of Jewish history. As a result, the Jewish people suffers today from a collective case of post-traumatic stress disorder. Consider: The most devastating tragedy in all of Jewish history was the destruction of the *Beit Ha-Mikdash,* the Holy Temple of Jerusalem, by the Romans in the year 70 CE. This devastation is matched by the Holocaust, the destruction of six million Jews by the Nazis. The most miraculous moment of redemption in all of Jewish history was the Exodus from Egypt. This miracle is matched by the rebirth of the State of Israel. The Exodus and the destruction of the Temple took place fifteen hundred years apart. The Holocaust and the birth of Israel took place within a decade, in the experience of one generation. How does one generation absorb such gyration? How do we make sense of such cataclysm?

Emerging from the trauma of the twentieth century, Jews stopped asking questions. Questions were too painful. The rabbi I grew up with was learned, pious, and wise, but he never talked about God from the bimah. He never talked about the meaning of Jewish history or the purpose of Jewish life. He never shared his beliefs. Years later, when I entered rabbinical school, I asked him why. It was too painful, he responded. In the shadow of the Holocaust, it was too difficult to open a discussion of belief and doubt, of suffering and meaning.

To numb the pain, the Jewish world adopted a single-minded ideology of survival. We called it "continuity." The ideology was best articulated by the philosopher Emil Fackenheim, who offered the idea that out of Auschwitz came a 614th commandment, the dominant obligation of our time: Don't let Hitler win. We don't know what to believe, he explained. All we know is that we are forbidden to hand Hitler a posthumous victory. So we silenced those who challenged and questioned. Instead, we kindled an explosion of collective creativity. Count up all the Jewish institutions built in the decades since World War II—all the synagogues and schools, all the agencies and organizations in North America, and all the infrastructure and institutions of the State of Israel. We didn't ask, Why? Or, For what ultimate purpose? Those questions hurt too much. In the face of so much Jewish death, we defined Jewish survival as a self-evident value and proceeded to build. We had no way to understand God's presence in the world, so we determined to be God's presence—to be the very providence and protection we prayed for. Where the angel of death had tread so heavily, we would re-create life.

Toward the end of the century, however, the numbness wore off. The ideology of survival wore thin. Young Jews began asking startling new questions: Why? Why survive? Why be Jewish? Why marry Jewish? Why raise children Jewish? Their parents responded by reflexively citing the horrors of the Holocaust, but the kids turned away unmoved. The double negation—anti-anti-Semitism—is not a foundation for Jewish life. The parents sent the kids to Israel to witness the miracle of the reborn Jewish state. But the kids asked, Why Israel? What is this to me? The community invested in more intensive and expensive forms of Jewish education—day schools and summer camps. But still the questions wouldn't go away.

We are not the first generation to ask these questions. These questions may be uncomfortable, but they are perennial. In our history, these are the very questions that signal the arrival of a new era in Jewish life—a moment of rebirth.

"WHY?" IS THE QUESTION

The Passover Haggadah imagines four children sitting with us at the Seder table. One child asks the "How" question: "How are the rites and rules of the Passover to be observed?" He is privileged as the Wise Child. His question is easy to answer—we just quote the text to him.

It is the second child who asks the harder question, the "Why" question: Why do we do this? What does this history teach us? How does the Seder narrative, the grand narrative of the Jewish people, find a place in our personal identity? What difference does all this make to us?

The Haggadah castigates him as the Wicked Child. (Presumably, he excludes himself by saying "to you." But go back and look at the Wise Child's question; he also says "to you." Somehow, he got away with it!) His question is personal and uncomfortable. We will find the answer in no text. His question demands a deep look into our own lives and values.

The Wise Child's question, the "How" question, reflects a certain historical moment—when identity is settled, authority is clear, and there is consensus about the meaning of Jewish life. The Wicked Child asks the question of our moment—the moment of revolution, discontinuity, transformation—when we search for new ways of understanding Jewish life and Jewish wisdom.

Then there is the last child at the Seder, the One Who Does Not Ask. This child is a mystery. After all, what Jewish child doesn't have at least one question? Not even, "When do we eat?" But we know him. He was yesterday's Wicked Child. Once castigated and chastened, he returns to the Seder to sit silently. He will not engage in the conversation. He has given up on us. He finds no meaning in our rites and traditions. He has given up on Judaism. So many contemporary Jews have followed his path. When asked their current religious affiliation in a recent survey, fully 22 percent of Jews, and some 38 percent of younger Jews, checked the box labeled "None."[1] "None-Jews." Not Orthodox, not Conservative, not Reform, not Zionists. Jews resigned to silence.

"Why?" is not a wicked question. "Why be Jewish?" grows from an intuition that there is something in Judaism we have not been shown. We intuit that there is more depth to Jewish life than superficial ethnic decoration. "Why be Jewish?" can be answered only by facing the Wicked Child's question: What does Judaism mean? What is its message? What does it do for us?

CHUTZPAH IS THE ANSWER

According to an ancient tradition, when the Israelites stood at Mount Sinai, God appeared to them as a mirror.[2] A mirror reflects back to us the truth about ourselves, a truth we may have forgotten or hidden from. The gift of Judaism is an understanding of what it means to be a human being—what we can do, what we can hope for, how we can live with purpose, what is expected of us. It is a celebration of human freedom, human possibility, and human responsibility. Judaism is a way to live a heroic life, to construct a life devoted to values that are eternal, values of ultimate significance. The reward of a Jewish life is walking the world with a profound faith that you matter, your life matters, your dreams matter.

I call this *chutzpah*.

The dictionary defines *chutzpah* as "unmitigated effrontery or impudence; gall; audacity; nerve." The writer Leo Rosten, in his classic *The Joys of Yiddish*, defines chutzpah as "incredible 'guts,' presumption plus arrogance such as no other word and no other language can do justice to." He evokes the clinical definition of *chutzpah*: "that quality enshrined in a man who, having killed his mother and father, throws himself on the mercy of the court because he is an orphan."[3]

The word *chutzpah* is actually much older than Yiddish. It is found in Talmudic literature. There, it also means "arrogant" or "insolent." But in the ancient texts, *chutzpah* has a second definition. It refers to irrepressible strength, irresistible boldness. The Jerusalem Talmud declared that the Land of Israel, despite all its devastation, remains irrepressibly fertile. The term used is *chutzpah*.[4] Likewise, the Talmud recognized that in every generation, there are certain human beings prepared to stand in the face of any power, even God, to champion life, demand justice, and appeal for compassion. These special souls are said to display "chutzpah even in the face of heaven—*chutzpah afilu kelapei shemaya.*"[5]

Chutzpah, in this definition, describes a rare quality of moral courage. This chutzpah is at the heart of Judaism. Chutzpah suggests the revolutionary conception of the human condition and our relationship to God offered by the Jewish tradition. The chutzpah of Judaism insists on the significance of human life, the possibilities of human goodness, and the depth of human responsibility to the world. It proclaims the dignity of being human and the possibilities of redemption. The message of Judaism is chutzpah.

The very assertion of this faith in human possibility was itself an act of chutzpah. Consider the irony: this tiny people who have known more suffering, persecution, and humiliation than any other people in human history—the very people who have been oppressed by the darkest evils promulgated by humanity—mustered the irrepressible courage to assert that human life is not absurd, that human dreams are not futile, that we yet possess the power to redeem our world.

This unique conception of human existence is the most important intellectual contribution of Jewish civilization to human culture. This is the precious gift of the Jews to humanity.

Such a powerful concept of human existence cannot be held in isolation from a correlate idea of the universe we inhabit. As Jews developed their unique ideas of human existence, they conceived of God in unique ways. Judaism is a theistic humanism. Only with a revolutionary idea of God could Jews maintain their revolutionary ideas of human life and its possibilities. Ethical monotheism is conventionally held to be the great contribution of Judaism, and that is certainly true. But we will argue that Jews came to ethical monotheism, and so many other remarkable theological innovations, to sustain their yet more remarkable concept of human existence.

To be sure, Judaism is an ocean of many currents and countercurrents. For every expression of chutzpah found in its sacred literature, there are equally compelling expressions of its opposite—humility, submission, the reality of our existential insignificance. Our task is not to summarize the entirety of a culture, but to trace one current of its wisdom—the tradition of theistic humanism within Jewish civilization—and to ascertain its implications for Jewish life today. This task was begun by many before us, many of whom were my teachers, including Rabbis Harold Schulweis, David Hartman (z"l), and Irving "Yitz" Greenberg. We will draw on their insights frequently. They understood that the history of chutzpah is the inner story of the Jewish people's soul. They perceived that tracing the history of chutzpah reveals the message of Judaism, its deepest purpose, and its most precious treasure. Chutzpah is the answer to the Wicked Child's question, and to our questions as well.

Chapter One

HOW TO ARGUE WITH GOD AND WIN

I love Jewish books. I attribute this to my fourth-grade Hebrew school teacher, who regularly banished me to the synagogue library. I wasn't a bad kid. On the contrary, I loved Hebrew school. But at the end of a full day of quietly paying attention to the lessons of "regular school," Hebrew school provided an ideal environment to meet, mix, and mingle. Scolded three or four times to sit quietly—"*Sheket*, Yitzchak, *sheket!*"—I would find myself sent to the library, where I learned to love Jewish books.

One time, the teacher caught me on the way out the door. "Yitzchak, go to the library!" she shouted. "But I want you do something there ... write a book report."

"Okay, fine. A book report. I can do that. I love books. Any particular book?"

"Yes," she smiled with a conspiratorial glee, "write a book report ... about the Bible."

"The Bible! How can I write a book report about the Bible?"

"It's a book, right? Then you can write a book report about it."

So off to the library I went. I found a copy of the Torah, took a piece of paper and a pencil, and began my book report.

Title: The Torah. So far, so good. Author—uh-oh. Just write: Unknown. Publisher: Jewish Publication Society. Describe the book: What is the setting? Who are the main characters? What is the plot? What happens in the book? What is the climax? How is it resolved? And finally, the all-important, Would you recommend this book to your friends?

The setting, the main characters, and especially, the plot. I have pondered these question a great deal since the fourth grade. Does the Bible have setting, character, plot? Does the Bible have a narrative arc? Does it tell a story? Typically, the Bible is not read that way. We read for individual nuggets of wisdom. We read a biblical story, a weekly portion, or a particular law. In the same way that we don't explore the deeper meanings of the Jewish tradition as an entirety, we don't read the whole expanse of the Bible for the totality of its narrative. And we miss its deepest truths.

WHAT IS THE BIBLE'S STORY?

Listen to an ancient myth: In the beginning, there was only water churning in chaos. From the chaos, the waters divided into two; the sweet, freshwater was known as the father god Apsu, and the bitter, salty ocean waters were known as Tiamat, the mother goddess. When they joined together, their comingling brought forth all the gods of the world—gods of sun, moon, and stars, gods of war and peace, fertility and barrenness, rain and drought. These gods were driven by passions and jealousies and lusts. Their carousing filled the world with noise and commotion, so much so that Father Apsu decided to kill them all and restore his quiet world. Learning of this plot against her children, Tiamat tipped off her son Ea, who used magic to put Apsu to sleep and then kill him. Enraged at the death of her husband, Tiamat herself turned against the younger gods. She created eleven monsters to destroy all the gods. The gods gathered anxiously in council. What could be done? Who dared resist the all-powerful mother goddess? Up stepped Marduk, god of thunder and lightning, who proposed a plan: he would fight the mother goddess on behalf of all the gods, and if victorious, he would be crowned king of the gods. The plan was quickly adopted and Marduk went off to battle against his mother.

The battle raged and raged until Marduk gained an upper hand. He pried open the mouth of the goddess, propped it with a thunder bolt, then cast another bolt of lethal lightning deep into Tiamat's belly. She died in agony. Marduk sliced her dead body in half. Half he placed above as the sky, and half he placed below as the earth.

Marduk celebrated his victory with a grand festival and was crowned king of the gods. But his rejoicing was short-lived. For it was Tiamat, the mother goddess, who provided sustenance for the gods. Once she was gone, there was no source of food.

Marduk set to work creating a suitable servant for the gods. He squeezed out the blood of the vanquished goddess into the mud of the river and formed the human. The human being was given the task of serving the gods—literally. Humanity was ordered to offer savory sacrifices whose smoke billowed toward the heavens and fed the appetites of the gods.

So goes the ancient Mesopotamian Creation myth *Enuma Elish*. Authored approximately 2000 BCE, this may have been Abraham's bedtime story.[1]

A myth is not a fairy tale, not a childish answer to mystery. Myth is a statement of a culture's deepest beliefs in the form of a story. It is not to be read in the past tense—"once upon a time." It is to be read in the present tense. It is a culture's statement of the truth of human existence.

What kind of world is described by the Mesopotamian Creation myth? The myth imagines a world populated by disparate powers divided against one another and locked in endless conflict.

The gods, driven by lusts, jealousies, and desires or by boredom and caprice, are pitted in perpetual warfare. It is a world without order, without stasis, without a moment of peace. The myth collapses the horizons of human possibility. In this world, the human being is a pitiful, powerless bystander. Anything a human being might dare to build will be snatched away or sullied by the uncontrolled impulses of the gods. We are children building sand castles by the seashore. The tide inevitably and irresistibly comes in and wipes away all our plans and projects, sullies our hopes, erases our dreams. The myth counsels passivity and surrender. Submit, warns the myth, acquiesce. Do as you are told, fulfill your role, serve the gods, ask for nothing in return, and perhaps you and your children might survive to see tomorrow.

This Mesopotamian myth was inscribed on clay tablets by its ancient authors and was discovered by archaeologists in 1849 when they uncovered the ancient city of Nineveh in Iraq. Because of this find, we can now understand something important about our Bible. The Hebrew Bible was a protest—an explicit rejection of this story. Our Bible was a polemic against this view of the world and its sad image of human existence.

> In the beginning God created heaven and earth—the earth being unformed and void, with darkness over the surface of the deep and a wind from God sweeping over the water—God said, "Let there be light"; and there was light. God saw that the light was good, and God separated the light from the darkness. God called the light Day, and the darkness God called Night. And there was evening and there was morning, a first day. (Genesis 1:1–5)

Compared to the Mesopotamian myth, Genesis is placid. It is dull. There is no battle. No struggle. No lusts, no passions, no blood. Instead, there is a majestic sense of order. Being rolls out according to a plan. Life begets life. Water gives way to land; land precedes vegetation, which precedes animal life, which anticipates the arrival of humanity. Within a world that is ordered, there is room for human beings to dream, to work, to build. The most important words of Genesis: "God saw that it was good." The world has possibilities. The future is inviting.

In the Mesopotamian story, the human being was created from the blood of the vanquished goddess to serve the appetites of her selfish children. Genesis chapter 1 parodies this notion and supplants it.

> And God said, "Let us make a human in our image, after our likeness. They shall rule the fish of the sea, the birds of the sky, the cattle, the whole earth, and all the creeping things that creep on earth." And God created the human in God's image, in the image of God did God create the human; male and female God created them. God blessed them and God said to them, "Be fertile and increase, fill the earth and master it; and rule the fish of the sea, the birds of the sky, and all the living things that creep on earth." (Genesis 1:26–28)

Just as in the Mesopotamian myth, the human being is created from the essence of the Divine. But in Genesis, the human being bears the image of the Creator and shares the power and responsibility for governing the world. In the Mesopotamian myth, the human being is object. The myth counsels obsequious passivity— sit quietly, don't dream, don't try too hard, don't care too much. In Genesis, the human being is subject, an actor in the drama of Creation. The human being is empowered to become a creator, partner with the divine Creator, and responsible for the destiny of Creation.

The Bible went to war with the Mesopotamian myth and its worldview. Not because it is empirically false. Myths are not disproven factually. The Bible stood against the myth because the moral capacity of the human being and the dignity of being human are threatened by this view of the world. The Mesopotamian myth offers a world closed to human dreams and aspirations, closed to human efforts.

The myth was born as the great Mesopotamian empires over-ran the villages, towns, and cities of the Middle East, amalgam-ating their cults and cultures into the imperial state. Stripped of their customs and traditions, the conquered peoples experienced the world as chaotic and strange. This insecurity is reflected in the myth. The myth projects an image of a world governed by merci-less, arbitrary, cruel forces of overwhelming power. There is no room in this world for hope. Fear rules this world.

The Bible understood that people driven by fear close up into a clinch. In the face of fear, conscience is occluded, com-passion withers and dies. Living in fear, we become indifferent to the needs of the other and deaf to moral ideals. We seek only protection for our own. Driven by fear, people will wrap them-selves in the cloak of victimhood, a cloak that covers any hor-ror. In the Bible's fourth chapter, Cain is so despondent that his offering is not accepted he kills his brother. Cain, the very first human being born into the world, feels himself a victim. As victim, he feels justified: "Adonai said to Cain, 'Where is your brother Abel?' And he said, 'I do not know. Am I my brother's keeper?'" (Genesis 4:9).

The British historian and moralist Lord Acton taught that power corrupts and absolute power corrupts absolutely. But pow-erlessness also corrupts. The sense of powerlessness inevitably leads to cynicism and despair. It despairs of the human capacity to shape the conditions of our own existence. It despairs of human dreams and hopes. It destroys the human soul. So the Bible struck out against this myth and offered a revolutionary idea of human existence: the human being is God's partner in creating the world. It was out of the Bible's struggle against the Mesopotamian myth and the world it described that chutzpah was born.

GOD'S ANTHROPOLOGY

The Bible, observed the twentieth-century philosopher and rabbi Abraham Joshua Heschel, is not our book about God. The Bible is God's anthropology—God's understanding of human beings.[2] The revolution of the Bible is not its concept of God, but its conception of the capacities and possibilities of human existence. Even though God is the central character of the biblical narrative, the Bible tells us very little about God. We are told nothing of God's origins, God's background or backstory. We know nothing of God's essence. All we know is that God dreams. And what is God's dream? A world of wholeness, a world that is one. The Bible is the story of God's dream. It is a drama told in three acts.

ACT ONE: MAN AND WOMAN

God creates a world and blesses it: "It is good." But God wants more than an inert, unconscious world. God wants a partner to enjoy this world, to share it and care for it. So God creates the human being. Unique among all creatures, the human being bears the divine image, so that like God, the human being dreams.

Oneness is the recurring theme of the Bible's story of Creation. There is unity between God and Creation. When God creates, God uses no process, materials, or plans. Creation is a spontaneous act of speaking reality into existence. There is no resistance in the act of creating; nothing pushes back against the will of the Creator. The opening phrase of Creation, "Let there be light—*Yehi or*" (Genesis 1:3), has no hard consonant through the final letter *reish*. God breathes existence into the world. The medieval mystics read this as a process of emanation—all that exists is a projection of

God, literally the exhaling of God's being into the world. All that is, is one with God.

There is oneness uniting God and the human being. In chapter 1 of Genesis, the human being is formed "in the image of God" (Genesis 1:27). In chapter 2, the human is animated by God's life-giving breath, *nishmat chayim* (Genesis 2:7). The human being carries God within. Some mystics suggested that the very name of God, which is held by tradition to be so sacred that it is never pronounced, is actually the very sound of the human breath. The four letters of the tetragrammaton, *Yud/Hei/Vav/Hei*, describe the sound of breath inhaled and exhaled. So wrote the psalmist, "Every breath praises God!" (Psalm 150:6). Every breath evokes the Divine. The Hebrew word for "soul," *neshamah*, is related to the word for "breath," *neshimah*. And the Hebrew for "wind," *ruach*, is the same as for "spirit." For that matter, in English, "spirit" is the root of both "inspiration" and "respiration."

Finally, there is oneness among human beings. In Genesis chapter 1, man and woman are created together and blessed together. In chapter 2, woman is created in answer to the man's deep need for companionship. She is taken from the rib—*tzeila*—or better, from the side of man. She is so much a reflection of him that the first time man speaks in the Bible, it is to extol his unity with woman: "*Zot ha-pa'am*—This one is bone of my bones and flesh of my flesh!" (Genesis 2:23).

God creates a remarkable place for this new human creature, a garden. The Garden of Eden is the epitome of God's dreams— a place of oneness, peace, coexistence, tranquility. Consider the image—a garden, not a palace, or a temple, or a city. A garden is an exquisite balance of nature and artifice. A garden is shaped by knowing hands, but it is animated by the energy of nature. A garden is dynamic; it is always growing and changing. It is always in need of care, cultivation, and work. A garden is a model of oneness: in a garden, every plant and animal is connected to every other aesthetically and organically. They depend on one another; they each have a role. The human being, created in the image of the Creator, is placed in this most perfect place, this Garden, and charged with the task of maintaining its dynamic perfection: *le-ovdah ule-shomrah*, says the Torah (Genesis 2:15), "to nurture and protect" God's creation. This is the specific role assigned by God to the human being. This is the purpose of human existence: to nurture and protect the oneness, the balance, the growth of the Garden.

But even in this place of perfection, the human being is not content. The Bible describes the paradox that is our human character: On the one hand, we crave oneness, connection, and intimacy. On the other hand, we have an inner drive toward individuation, freedom, and independence. Human development is the dynamic between these two poles. As we mature, we let go of bonds to become the individuals we are meant to be, and then we unite in new attachments to form family and community. "Hence, a man leaves his father and his mother and clings to his wife, so that they become one flesh" (Genesis 2:24). Because of this dynamic, the place of God-given perfection is too confining. Created in the image of the Creator, human beings need to fashion their own reality, to determine their own destiny. The man and the woman choose autonomy over obedience, and they betray the partnership—they disobey God's rule.

Bewildered and disappointed, God expels them from the Garden and grants them their freedom. But that freedom comes at a price: an end to the perfect oneness of the Garden. The curses doled out at the end of Genesis chapter 3 are not punishments, but the consequences of choosing individuation over oneness. Man and woman will no longer enjoy the unities of Eden. Henceforth, human beings will seek oneness with God but never fully achieve it. They will find nature an adversary, yielding its bounty only sparingly. Try as they might, they will never again know perfect oneness with one another. Men and women will find one another endlessly mysterious. And in the end, they will experience the ultimate separation—they will know death.

Here is the most interesting detail of the story: God banishes the human being, but God doesn't destroy the Garden. The Garden becomes inaccessible but not invisible. Rather, it lives very visibly, at the very center of the human world. It lives at the very heart of human dreams. Genesis offers this consolation: Eden exists. Eden is real. Within the brokenness and frustration of daily experience, there always lives the possibility of oneness, peace, and harmony. It is neither inconceivable nor impossible. But it is just out of reach at this moment. Learning how to reenter Eden, how to regain its peace and oneness, is the eternal task of Jewish faith. It is our eternal journey.

ACT TWO: NOAH

Outside the Garden, the human being turns away from God's dream of oneness. Individuation goes wild, and over the next ten generations humanity descends from disobedience to murder and wanton violence. God gives up on humanity altogether and decides to destroy them all and wipe the world clean. Just then, God's eye catches sight of one man, a man of goodness. God finds Noah, *ish tzaddik,* a righteous man. And God decides to start over.

If God can't create a human being to share the dream, perhaps God can choose one, choose someone committed to the divine dream of a world of oneness. The world is wiped clean by the Flood. But after departing from the ark, Noah disappoints God as well. His children turn away from God's dreams and fill the world again with corruption and violence. Once again God is disappointed with humanity. With all God's power, God could not create a worthy partner. With all God's vision, God could not choose a partner. Perhaps, God can teach a human being to cherish the dream of oneness.

ACT THREE: ABRAHAM

Adonai said to Abram, "Go forth from your native land and from your father's house to the land that I will show you.

I will make of you a great nation,

And I will bless you;

I will make your name great,

And you: Be a blessing!

I will bless those who bless you

And curse him that curses you;

And blessed in you shall be all the families of the earth."

(Genesis 12:1–3)

God's strategy: Take a man and remove him from his culture. Strip him of his identity, his power, position, prestige, and patrimony. Then remake him into a vessel of divine blessing: "Be a blessing. Bring blessing to all the families of the earth."

Pay careful attention to the commandment. God doesn't say, "Be a blessing to Me." God doesn't demand Abraham's reverence, worship, or submission. God only asks: Walk with Me. Be My partner. Nurture and protect My world. Share My dream. Bring blessing into My world. Abraham's children are not even required to obey God. God never asks for that. What they have to do is share God's dream—pursue it and fight for it. They must be a vessel for the divine dream among the families of humanity.

Typically, we think of God in vertical metaphors. God is up there; we are down here. "Our Father in heaven—*Avinu shebashamayim*." God is exalted; humans are humbled. But the Bible's idea of covenant turns this vertical image horizontal. God needs this human being. God empowers the human being. The human is elevated to become a partner in realizing the divine dream. How far will the Bible go in reimagining the relationship?

One day, three visitors arrive at Abraham's tent. It is soon apparent that they are angels. The first announces the coming birth of Abraham and Sarah's son Isaac. The other two have a more fateful mission.

> The men set out from there and looked down toward Sodom, Abraham walking with them to see them off. Now Adonai had said, "Shall I hide from Abraham what I am about to do, since Abraham is to become a great and populous nation and all the nations of the earth are to bless themselves by him? For I have singled him out, that he may instruct his children and his posterity to keep the way of Adonai by doing what is just and right, in order that Adonai may bring about for Abraham what God has promised him." Then Adonai said, "The outrage of Sodom and Gomorrah is so great, and their sin so grave! I will go down to see whether they have acted altogether according to the outcry that has reached Me; if not, I will take note." (Genesis 18:16–21)

The Bible imagines God ruminating: "Shall I hide from Abraham what I am about to do?" The ostensible answer is, Of course You should, You're God! God is not accountable to anyone! But here is the revolution in the biblical idea of covenant: once God enters into partnership, God indeed becomes accountable. If Abraham is to promote God's justice in the world, to advocate and teach it, that justice must become transparent. God and Abraham must share a common moral language. And God can be held accountable to that same standard of justice. God must operate in the world according to that standard. Once God enters into partnership, God is open to questioning.

The men went on from there to Sodom, while Abraham
remained standing before Adonai. Abraham came forward
and said, "Will You sweep away the innocent along with the
guilty? What if there should be fifty innocent within the city;
will You then wipe out the place and not forgive it for the
sake of the innocent fifty who are in it? Far be it from You
to do such a thing, to bring death upon the innocent as well
as the guilty, so that innocent and guilty fare alike. Far be it
from You! Shall not the Judge of all the earth deal justly?"
And Adonai answered, "If I find within the city of Sodom fifty
innocent ones, I will forgive the whole place for their sake."
Abraham spoke up, saying, "Here I venture to speak to my
Lord, I who am but dust and ashes: What if the fifty innocent
should lack five? Will You destroy the whole city for want of
the five?" And God answered, "I will not destroy if I find forty-
five there." But he spoke to God again, and said, "What if forty
should be found there?" And God answered, "I will not do
it, for the sake of the forty." And he said, "Let not my Lord
be angry if I go on: What if thirty should be found there?"
And God answered, "I will not do it if I find thirty there."
And he said, "I venture again to speak to my Lord: What if
twenty should be found there?" And God answered, "I will not
destroy, for the sake of the twenty." And he said, "Let not my
Lord be angry if I speak but this last time: What if ten should
be found there?" And God answered, "I will not destroy, for
the sake of the ten." When Adonai had finished speaking to
Abraham, God departed; and Abraham returned to his place.
(Genesis 18:22–33)

This is the epitome of biblical chutzpah. The human being dresses
God down in no unsubtle terms. "Far be it from You to do such
a thing, to bring death upon the innocent as well as the guilty,

so that innocent and guilty fare alike. Far be it from You!" The original Hebrew *chalilah lecha* is actually much more earthy than the literary "Far be it from You!" The connotation is closer to my grandmother's Yiddish curse whenever I'd beat up my little brother. She'd shake her head and whisper, "*Shonda! Herpah!*— Shame on You! You're better than that!" Abraham gives voice to his utter disappointment in God's betrayal of their shared ideal of justice: How could You, God, even think of acting in such a way that so blurs the moral distinction between good and evil, between innocence and guilt? Is that the world You designed? A world without distinction between right and wrong? Shame on You! You're better than that!

Even more remarkable, God accepts it. God relents. But the Bible isn't finished. The Bible wants to play out the drama to its end. So Abraham continues bargaining. Fifty becomes forty-five. Forty-five slips to forty; forty to thirty; thirty to twenty; twenty to ten. And only then does Abraham stop. Ten, it seems, is the minimum quorum for nurturing moral personality. The story has a quality of the absurd, the ridiculous. What kind of God is this? What religious universe is being described by this story? A God who accepts human rebuke is a God more committed to teaching an ideal of justice than in maintaining a divine prerogative of authority. Faithfulness to the divine dream takes priority over deference before God's majesty. Nothing, it seems, is more sacred than divine justice, not even God's own authority. This is a celebration of chutzpah, of covenantal audacity.

To gain a sense of this audacity, contrast this story with another famous biblical tale, the story of Job.

> There was a man in the land of Uz named Job. That man was
> righteous and good; he revered God and kept away from evil.
> Seven sons and three daughters were born to him.... That

man was wealthier than anyone in the East.... One day the angels presented themselves before Adonai, and the Adversary [*Ha-Satan*] came along with them. Adonai said to the Adversary, "Where have you been?" The Adversary answered Adonai, "I have been roaming over the earth." Adonai said to the Adversary, "Have you noticed My servant Job? There is no one like him on earth, a blameless and upright man who reveres God and keeps away from evil!" "God? Why, it is You who have fenced him round, him and his household and all that he has. You have blessed his efforts so that his possessions spread out in the land. But lay Your hand upon all that he has and he will surely curse You to Your face." Adonai replied to the Adversary, "See, all that he has is in your power; only do not lay a hand on him." The Adversary departed from the presence of Adonai. (Job 1:1–3, 1:6–12)

God wagers with Satan, and Job loses everything—his wealth, his health, his children, and his faith. You've heard of the "patience of Job"? That lasts only two chapters. For the next thirty-six chapters, Job screams in agony and rage toward heaven, "Why me?" But God doesn't answer. God feels obligated to explain God's plans to Abraham. God feels no such obligation to Job.

Withering under the burden of so much undeserved suffering, Job gives up on divine justice. He flings toward heaven words that specifically contrast with Abraham's words:

Wise of heart and mighty in power—
  Whoever challenged God and came out whole?...
  Who can say to God, "What are You doing?"
  ... I am distraught; I am sick of life.
  It is all one; therefore I say,
  "God destroys the blameless and the guilty.
  (Job 9:4, 9:12, 9:21–22)

Job experiences the amoral world that Abraham so feared and despised—a world without moral distinctions, a world where human action and aspiration mean nothing, a world of undeserved suffering and meaningless destruction, a world not unlike the world of the Mesopotamian Creation myth.

Eventually, at the end of the book, God responds to Job. But unlike Abraham, God listens to none of Job's charges. God intimidates and humiliates Job. Appearing in a tempest, a hurricane, God takes Job on a tour of the world of nature to humble and to silence him.

> Then Adonai replied to Job out of the tempest and said:
>> Who is this who darkens counsel,
>> Speaking without knowledge?
>> Gird your loins like a man;
>> I will ask and you will inform Me.
>> Where were you when I laid the earth's foundations?
>> Speak if you have understanding.
>> Do you know who fixed its dimensions
>> Or who measured it with a line?
>> Onto what were its bases sunk?
>> Who set its cornerstone ...
>> Who closed the sea behind doors...?
>> Have you ever commanded the day to break,
>> Assigned the dawn its place...?
>> Do you know the laws of heaven
>> Or impose its authority on earth?
>> (Job 38:1–6, 38:8, 38:12, 38:33)

In Abraham, God found a partner for the fulfillment of a divine dream, a world of justice and right. In Job, God sees only a nuisance to be silenced and removed. "Who are you?" Job is asked again and again. "Who are you to challenge God? Who are you?" Finally, and tragically, Job is cowed into surrender.

> Job said in reply to Adonai:
>> I know that You can do everything,
>> That nothing you propose is impossible for You.
>> Who is this who obscures counsel without knowledge?
>> Indeed, I spoke without understanding
>> Of things beyond me, which I did not know.
>> Hear now, and I will speak;
>> I will ask, and You will inform me.
>> I had heard You with my ears,
>> But now I see You with my eyes;
>> Therefore, I recant and relent,
>> Being but dust and ashes.
> (Job 42:1–6)

In only two places in the Hebrew Bible is the human being described as "dust and ashes"—the stories of Abraham and Job. In the story of Abraham, the phrase is ironic. It comes just as Abraham is about to score his moral victory against God. In Job, the same expression is the resigned expression of human surrender. Job is so overwhelmed, he doesn't recognize the logical inconsistency of God's answer. Job questions God's justice. God responds by demonstrating immeasurable power. But that power so humbles Job, he ceases to question. Job concludes that he and God live in different moral worlds. To question divine morality is futile—what is justice in a human perspective is not justice in the divine perspective. He recants and relents and resigns. He surrenders his quest to understand divine morality. There are those who admire Job for his ethic of acceptance and the equanimity it brings. But from the perspective of Abraham, Job's surrender can only be seen as a tragic defeat.

Two biblical characters; two religious personalities; two different universes. What is the difference between them? Why does the Bible offer us these two portraits?

Abraham challenges God. His challenge is accepted by God. Job challenges. His challenge and his spirits are crushed. The name "Job" is not Hebrew. It is an old name in a much older language. In most ancient Near Eastern languages, "Job" means "Everyman." He is John Doe, the cipher for the common human experience. As God took Job on a tour of Creation, Everyman meets God in nature. Nature displays power and majesty, but no morality. Nature knows no justice. Cancer, earthquakes, tornadoes, tsunamis destroy indiscriminately. What good does it do to rail against the chaos of nature? In the face of nature's moral indifference, wisdom dictates an attitude of acceptance. At most, we might aspire to gain the power to exert some control over nature through science.

Abraham is different. He is covenanted. He meets God in their shared vision of justice. His is the task of bringing divine justice into the world. Abraham is invited to expect more, to demand more of God and the world. For Abraham, surrender is a sin. To accept the world as it is—to declare, "What is, is what is meant to be"—is blasphemy. It is to surrender his role as partner with the Divine in bringing oneness back into the world. The unrelenting insistence on justice—even if it means challenging God—marks Abraham as a singular religious hero. It is chutzpah at its finest.

In the juxtaposition of Abraham and Job, we are offered two models of the religious personality, two possibilities for walking the world. Job embodies an ethic of acceptance. In resignation, he surrenders his expectation that God's world ought to be just. Through that resignation, he accepts what is, and he finds peace. Abraham is the embodiment of chutzpah. His life will not be peaceful; there is no equanimity in his stance toward the world. He will demand justice and risk everything in the pursuit of what's right. But having fought valiantly for the divine dream of justice, he will find dignity and purpose.

Of course, Abraham will have his own Job-experience. A few chapters after challenging God over the fate of Sodom, God demands the ultimate sacrifice from Abraham:

> Some time afterward, God put Abraham to the test. God said to him, "Abraham," and he answered, "Here I am." And God said, "Take your son, your favored one, Isaac, whom you love, and go to the land of Moriah, and offer him there as a burnt offering on one of the heights that I will point out to you." (Genesis 22:1–2)

Abraham obeys. Where is his argument now? Where is his chutzpah? Perhaps, he was able to argue on behalf of others but not for himself. But having waited his entire adult life for the arrival of this son, has he no response? Typically, the Bible shows us the exterior of characters and leaves it to the reader to fill in the emotional interior. It is left to us to imagine Abraham's heart. Is he anguished? Resigned? Combative? Numb? Rabbis in every generation have commented on this story. One of the most remarkable comes from *Midrash Tanchuma* and is retold exquisitely by Elie Wiesel. This midrash focuses on the story's moment of truth and the anomalies embedded within that text:

> When God sent the angel to restrain Abraham, he refused to heed the call.
>
> "God Himself ordered me to sacrifice my son, it is up to Him to rescind the order!"
>
> And so God himself comes to retract the commandment. But Abraham struggles to continue. With the knife at the throat of his son, he begins to argue:
>
> "I swear I shall not leave the altar, Lord, before I speak my mind."

"Speak," said God.

"Did You not promise me that my descendants would be as numerous as the stars in the sky?"

"Yes, I did promise you that."

"And whose descendants will they be? Mine? Mine alone?"

"No," said God, "they will be Isaac's as well."

"And didn't You also promise me that they would inherit the earth?"

"Yes, I promised you that too."

"And whose descendants will they be? Mine alone?"

"No," said God, "they will be Isaac's as well."

"Well then, my Lord," said Abraham, "I could have pointed out to You before that Your order contradicted Your promise. I could have spoken up; I didn't. I contained my grief and held my tongue. In return, I want You to make me the following promise: that when, in the future, my children and my children's children throughout the generations will act against Your law and against Your will, You will also say nothing and forgive them."

"So be it," God agreed. "Let them but retell this tale, and they will be forgiven."[3]

None of this occurs in the biblical text. On the contrary, in this story, the Bible casts a spell of silence upon Abraham. The great Danish philosopher Søren Kierkegaard regarded this silence as the highest paradigm of faith. The loyal "knight of faith," Kierkegaard taught, Abraham gives up everything, including the dictates of his own conscience, to follow the will of God in silent obedience. The Rabbis of the midrash disagree.

In their view, obedience to God is expressed not in silent submission, but in the protest of an Abraham who expects more from God. The Rabbis would rather have an Abraham who is loyal to God's justice than an Abraham submissive to God's authority. They so cherished the chutzpah of the Sodom story, they superimposed that Abraham onto this story (that's chutzpah!) and imagined the argument Abraham should have had with God. In fact, as Wiesel tells it, the story is turned completely upside down— instead of God testing Abraham, the Rabbis of the midrash would have Abraham testing God.

This midrash replays the story of Job, but with Abraham as its hero. Given Job's circumstances, the Rabbis wonder, what would Abraham have done? And what would have happened to him? Job relented. He acquiesced. Job represents acceptance. Abraham fights on for justice. And in the end, it is God who relents. Abraham succeeds in wrestling a significant concession from God: "Let them but retell this tale, and they will be forgiven." Which tale? Not the Bible's story of submission, but the midrash tale of chutzpah. The Rabbis imagined that God so cherishes Abraham's chutzpah that rehearsing the story of Abraham's challenge draws God's heart closer to Abraham's children, close enough to erase any sin or transgression that might separate them. The memory of Abraham's chutzpah awakens God's love in each subsequent generation. Conversely, telling the story awakens within the hearts of Abraham's progeny the possibility of unity with divine purposes and the courage to demand justice from the world. Thus, the merit of Abraham's chutzpah spills over into all the generations of his descendants.

Abraham is our spiritual ancestor. All our stories are contained in his. Abraham is the father of chutzpah, a chutzpah expressed in the moral courage to stand before any authority and demand justice. Even God. The God Abraham taught us to worship not only tolerates this challenge, but cherishes it. For Abraham's God, the expression of chutzpah is itself a form of worship.

Chapter Two

THE ROAD TO EDEN

The Nazis took my uncle Henry at the very beginning of the war. He survived more than five years working as a slave for the SS. Young and strong, he was a carpenter, and the Nazis needed carpenters. They moved him from camp to camp until finally he arrived at Auschwitz. He was part of the forced labor crew that built the camp. When the Allies advanced, he was taken on a death march through the Polish winter into Germany. In 1945, he was liberated by the American army. He came to America, married my aunt, and became part of our family.

For as long as I can remember, Uncle Henry never spoke about these experiences. We knew that he had been in the camps from the numbers on his arm and from the peculiar way he slept so still, as if he were still hiding. But he would never reveal to any of us where he'd been, what he'd seen. He never spoke of any of it.

It was Elie Wiesel who opened my uncle's heart. Wiesel came to lecture at a local university, and my aunt and uncle went to hear him. Wiesel spoke about his time in Auschwitz. Every event Wiesel described, Uncle Henry had personally witnessed. Following the lecture, he approached Wiesel. They talked together in the deserted lecture hall for hours. Finally, Wiesel asked my uncle, "Have you told your children?" And my uncle sheepishly replied that he did not, he could not. "You must," Wiesel admonished, "for if you don't, they will never really believe it happened! They will never learn! You must be a witness. That's why we survived—to tell the story, to teach them!"

After a Passover meal some months later, he sat us down, and for more than three hours, Uncle Henry told us his story: How the Nazis rounded up the Jews of his town and made a selection—who would live and who would die. The cattle cars, the brutal slavery, the camps, Auschwitz, the death march, and finally, his liberation. When at last he finished, we sat in silence for some time. We finally mustered the nerve to ask why he'd waited all these years to share this. He looked at us with an embarrassed expression. "I was afraid you wouldn't understand. How could you understand? You grew up here, in freedom and safety. You have never felt real hunger or cold, you've never known fear or hate. How could you understand?" So then, why tell us now? "Because Wiesel is right. If you don't hear it from me, you'll never really believe that it happened, that it was real. You will never learn. I am a witness. It happened, worse than I've told you. Know that it happened. Learn from it!"

The survivors of the Holocaust are precious and rare. They are our witnesses. Their eyes saw what human eyes should never see; their ears heard what human ears should never hear. They know the darkest evil with an immediacy that no soul should be able to bear. And yet, most did not surrender to cynicism or bitterness or death. They didn't give up their hopes. Where did they find the courage to return to the world, to build families and communities, to live and work and love again?

Following his revelation to us, my uncle became an ambassador of the Holocaust. He visited every high school in his home state of New Jersey, telling his story. And at the end of his talk, he would demand that the kids promise they would build a different world. He built Auschwitz, the kingdom of death, he told them; theirs is the task of building a kingdom of life.

This is more than a survivor's resilience. It is an expression of something deeper. God commanded Abraham, "Be a blessing!" (Genesis 12:2). Jewish tradition has always held that this commandment is to be fulfilled, not in the private recesses of the soul, but in the real world, in history. Jews don't believe in the salvation of the soul without the redemption of the world. But history, it has been observed, is a charnel house of carnage and absurdity. History is a nightmare. How does a people remain faithful to its mission to bring blessing to the families of the earth when it finds itself cast into an endless pit of hatred and violence? To experience the darkest evil and not to give up on the world reflects qualities of courage and character we call "chutzpah."

Where did we learn this chutzpah? A place called Egypt.

EGYPT: LIVING AND RELIVING EDEN'S OPPOSITE

> A new king arose over Egypt who did not know Joseph. And he said to his people, "Look, the Israelite people are much too numerous for us. Let us deal shrewdly with them, so that they may not increase; otherwise in the event of war they may join our enemies in fighting against us and rise from the ground." So they set taskmasters over them to oppress them with forced labor.... Ruthlessly they made life bitter for them with harsh labor at mortar and bricks and with all sorts of tasks in the field. (Exodus 1:8–13)

The Garden of Eden represents the divine dream of a world of oneness and peace; Egypt is its diametric opposite. In Egypt, the people Israel entered a nightmare of slavery, brutality, and death. In Eden, the human being was celebrated as a uniquely precious creature fashioned in the image of the Creator. In Eden, we were one with God and one with each other. Egypt is the symbol of individuation taken to its more grotesque extreme—the enslavement of another. Slavery is the deconstruction of all that is human—the total objectification of another human being. The slave is not human, not animal, not even an object of any real value, but the embodiment of a quantity of labor. Slavery is the condition of total human insignificance, social invisibility—to be unseen, unheard, unrecognized, unacknowledged, unvalued. Over time, slaves internalize this condition. They cease to see themselves as human beings enslaved and come to believe this is their natural, ordained, deserved condition. All the dignity and possibility of Eden is lost to them. They cherish only one dream—let tomorrow's suffering be no worse than yesterday's.

Egypt was God's classroom, part of a radical pedagogy: to create an entire people committed to Abraham's covenant—to pursue the divine dream of justice in the world, a people prepared to serve as a vessel of divine blessing to all humanity—God brings Israel to a world of ultimate cruelty, darkness, and evil. To cherish the dream of Eden, we must live the nightmare of Egypt.

And not just once. "In every generation, each person must see him- or herself as if he or she were redeemed from Egypt."[1] This is radical. On Thanksgiving, Americans may remember the experience of their Pilgrim ancestors. But for Judaism, memory alone is insufficient. It isn't enough just to remember the Exodus from Egypt. It isn't enough to commemorate our escape from slavery or to celebrate our freedom. We have to be there personally and feel it. We must experience these events and become witnesses. Collective history must become personal memory. And so we return to Egypt every year at Passover. Every year, we eat what they ate. History must be ingested. We choke down the flat dry bread of slaves. We swallow the bitterness of slavery mellowed only by the sweet promise of redemption. We taste the tears.

Why such a demand? Why, of all the memories, are we bidden to return, year after year, to such a bitter moment? To show us what is at stake in human history. Human existence is poised between two poles—Egypt and Eden—between the nightmare and the dream. We move the world in one direction or the other. This is the radical responsibility laid upon those who count themselves among Abraham's descendants: bring the world to the oneness of Eden or watch it fall into the horror of Egypt.

The Hasidic master Rabbi Nachman of Breslov taught that Pharaoh was not an earthly king but a symbol for the human ego. Taught Rabbi Nachman, we are all enslaved to a Pharaoh within. The human heart is driven by jealousy and fear, by greed for gain and lust for power. Having chosen individuation as our way of being, we fall into servitude to the appetites and demands and impulses of the ego. We worship the projections of ego. It takes a radical pedagogy to liberate us and to awaken us to a different vision of human being—to the possibility of a different world, the vision of Eden's oneness. And so every year the Jewish collective experience begins again in Egypt.

At the Passover Seder, the child asks, "On all other nights we eat leavened bread; why on this night do we eat only matzah?" Matzah has two meanings at the Seder table. At the beginning of the Seder, it is the dry, tasteless bread of slaves. At the end, it is the flat bread taken in haste by slaves anxious to escape their bondage. This dual meaning attaches to many of the Seder symbols. *Charoset*, the sweet relish served at the Seder table, is said to resemble the mortar used by slaves in the construction of Pharaoh's monuments. Later in the Seder, it will be eaten with the bitter *maror*, so that the bitter taste of slavery is mellowed by the sweet anticipation of redemption. The holiday itself bears both meanings. On this night, we revisit the horror of slavery to know the bitter humiliation of the slave. And then (just before dinner is served) we cross the Red Sea, a step ahead of the chariots of Pharaoh. Reaching the other side, we celebrate the exhilaration of freedom.

Splitting the Sea

> Then Moses held out his arm over the sea and Adonai drove
> back the sea with a strong east wind all that night, and turned
> the sea into dry ground. The waters were split, and the Israelites
> went into the sea on dry ground, the waters forming a wall for
> them on their right and on their left. The Egyptians came in
> pursuit after them into the sea, all of Pharaoh's horses, char-
> iots, and horsemen.... Moses held out his arm over the sea,
> and at daybreak the sea returned to its normal state, and the
> Egyptians fled at its approach. But Adonai hurled the Egyptians
> into the sea.... Thus Adonai delivered Israel that day from the
> Egyptians.... Then Moses and the Israelites sang this song to
> Adonai. (Exodus 14:21–23, 14:27, 14:30, 15:1)

The Exodus narrative teaches us to hold two truths: Evil is real;
we have felt its cruelty. But redemption is also real; we have sung
its song. Only when we know the harsh brutality of slavery will
we become consumed with the divine demand for justice and
rise to become partners in reaching for the dream of Eden. And
only as participants in liberation, only when our feet are muddied
from crossing the Red Sea bed, will we shake off all our cynicism,
despair, and inertia, to gain the chutzpah to truly believe that the
world can be healed. In Egypt, we were liberated from physical
slavery. At the sea, we were liberated from the slavery of the spirit.

Before there was anything, relates Genesis, there was water.
In Genesis, water represents chaos. To create a habitable world, a
world where life might thrive, God split the waters and uncovered
dry land. The chaos of the waters gives way to the order of the cosmos. In Exodus, God again splits the waters, this time to create history. History emerges out of the chaos of human events. History is
not the random interplay of blind power, politics, and economics.
History has order and meaning. History is a journey from Egypt

to Eden. At the Red Sea, Israel learned that history has purpose and God has aspirations for human history. God cares. The divine dream is to bring humanity out of the nightmare of Egypt and into the light of Eden.

But there is something missing in the Torah's story of the splitting of the sea. The story has suspense, breathtaking excitement, miraculous special effects—it is certainly the most cinematic episode in the Hebrew Bible. But something is missing. The Rabbis of the midrash noticed this. So just as with the story of Abraham and Isaac, they retold the story. They told the story as it *should* have been told.

In the Rabbis' telling, Moses leads the people to the banks of the sea. Then they hear the hoofbeats of Pharaoh's approaching armies. The people cry out to Moses. Moses prays to God. He is told to hold his arm over the sea, which will cause the sea to split. And all this he does, exactly as he is commanded ... but the sea doesn't split. He tries again, but the sea still does not move. Now he becomes nervous. He tries to recall the exact words of God, the exact instructions. Once again, he holds his arm over the waters. And once again they do not move. Moses panics. The people panic. Everyone is immobilized with fear. And no one knows what to do.

No one, that is, except one man. One man perceives what even Moses our teacher cannot. His name is Nachshon ben Aminadav, one of the princes of the tribes of Israel. Nachshon understands that God is waiting. God sent Moses. And God brought the plagues. And God led them out of Egypt. But now God is waiting for the people to take some role in their own redemption. God, Nachshon understands, will not split the sea until someone moves—moves toward his or her own redemption—until someone is ready to risk his or her own life to bring salvation.

So Nachshon ben Aminadav jumps into the waters of the Red Sea.

At first, everyone looks at him with wonder and awe. "What are you doing?" his family shouts. But he pays no heed; he knows exactly what he is doing. And he wades out farther until the water covers his knees. His family screams and shouts and begs him to return, but he goes farther, until the water covers his waist. And now, everyone stands in silence and watches. He wades farther, until the water covers his shoulders. And then a few more steps, and he disappears under the water. And only when the water covers his nostrils and Nachshon can no longer breathe—only when he begins to drown—then, and only then, does the sea split and Israel cross in safety.

None of this is in the Torah. In the Torah, the people Israel are passive observers—objects, not subjects of the drama. The narrative is all about God—God's glory at the expense of the Egyptians, God's final victory over Pharaoh. The Rabbis of this midrash objected: this is not how God works in history. There is something missing from the Torah's narrative—God's human partner. Redemption is possible, assert the Rabbis, even immanent. But redemption will not arrive without a substantial commitment of human effort. Waiting passively on the side of the sea will not bring deliverance. Even prayer does not produce salvation. Redemption comes only when human beings jump into the cold and swirling waters of history. The sea splits only when someone is ready to go "all in"—to devote body and soul to the task of salvation.

Sometimes the sea doesn't split. Sometimes Pharaoh's armies catch us before we step across. The Rabbis knew this too well. But they would rather believe in a God who depends on a human partner in shaping history than a God who relegates the human being to the passive status of bystander. Slaves are passive. Free people demand the dignity of sharing in the creation of their own destiny.

Genesis recounts the creation of the universe. Exodus describes the creation of a covenanted people. The slavery of Egypt and the miraculous liberation were only the first steps in the process of shaping a people into a vessel of divine blessing. Crossing the sea does not take us directly to the Promised Land. On the far side of the sea, Israel began a journey across the forbidding wilderness of Sinai.

TAKING THE JOURNEY, EDUCATING THE SOUL

Every generation has its revolutionaries—passionate spirits who fervently believe that one apocalyptic "big bang" can forever liberate the human spirit and transform the human condition. Revolutionary passions are enchanting, their enthusiasms disarming, and their songs inspiring. But their theories are misguided. The Bible shares the revolutionary's faith in the possibilities of human dreams. But the Bible is realistic and humble about the limitations of human character. Human beings don't change all at once. A people enslaved does not become free overnight. Even the most spectacular of divine miracles cannot extinguish the fear that controls the slave's existence and defines the slave's vision of life. A slave is trained to always look down. The cataclysm of the splitting of the sea cannot by itself lift the slave's vision nor liberate the inner life. Outer chains can be broken with one sure blow. Inner chains take much longer. Three days after witnessing the miracles at the sea, the people Israel begin to complain, something they do very well.

> In the wilderness, the whole Israelite community grumbled against Moses and Aaron. The Israelites said to them, "If only we had died by the hand of Adonai in the land of Egypt, when we sat by the fleshpots, when we ate our fill of bread! For you have brought us out into this wilderness to starve this whole congregation to death." (Exodus 16:2–3)

Liberating the human spirit from ingrained fears, appetites, and resentments is harder than liberating slaves from a Pharaoh. It takes more than the apocalyptic moment. A new pattern of daily behavior must be internalized, a pattern that slowly changes human responses and attitudes. The story of this process occupies much of the Torah after the Exodus. It is the story of the wilderness journey.

The Torah is a road story. The road is the most powerful motif in Western literature. Everyone tells road stories—Homer, Chaucer, Melville, Tolkien, even *The Wizard of Oz*. The road depicts the development of human character. The road is the unfolding of the inner life. Dorothy doesn't only find the Emerald City; she also finds herself and her truth. She may return home to Kansas, but she returns transformed.

The Torah is the archetype of all road stories. The journey from Egypt to the Promised Land represents the human journey from smallness to greatness, from selfishness and fear to compassion and solidarity. This road story is the master narrative of Jewish life. It is recounted daily in the recitation of the Song of the Sea incorporated into the daily prayer service. It is recounted weekly in the portions of the Torah. It is recounted yearly in the cycle of Jewish festivals—Passover, celebrating the liberation from Egypt; Shavuot, celebrating the revelation at Mount Sinai; Sukkot, celebrating the trek across the wilderness.

The Torah is brutally honest in its portrayal of human moral deficiency. It spares nothing in describing the flawed human material out of which God wishes to shape a holy people. In the wilderness of Sinai, we meet the wildness of the human soul. On this road, all our inner demons are revealed—fear, envy, rivalry, zealotry. Only slowly will we come to know our own possibilities and come to share the dreams of the God who liberated us.

Israel begins its national life as morally defective as any people has ever been. The chutzpah of the Torah is its unyielding faith in the power of human transformation. The Torah is not a story about our faith in God, but of God's faith in us. The Torah attests to God's faith that a band of ex-slaves, as narrow-minded, contentious, and fearful as human beings can get, can yet be transformed into agents of blessing. The wilderness is where God's faith is tested.

The Torah's account of the trek across the wilderness is the story of Israel's spiritual and moral growth. The journey across the wilderness is the journey of the soul's education. The Torah's narrative of the arduous trek is woven together with the narrative of revelation, God's instructions.

The principal task of Torah is to teach us to move forward. Torah offers a map across this wilderness. Mitzvot are signposts along the way. Traditionally, *mitzvah* means "commandment." In a life of tradition, the observance of mitzvot signifies a gesture of obedience toward a commanding God. But in the context of covenantal partnership, a partnership of shared dedication to the task of bringing divine blessing into the world, mitzvah means more than commandment, and observance means more than obedience. Through the eyes of chutzpah, mitzvot are the discrete acts that bring our shared dream into reality. Mitzvot designate the individual steps that move the human being and the human community from Egypt to Eden. Mitzvot are revealed and they are sacred, not because they were cast down from above upon a submissive people, but because they reveal the way forward in our shared journey toward the world of blessing.

> You shall not wrong a stranger or oppress him, for you were strangers in the land of Egypt. You shall not ill-treat any widow or orphan. (Exodus 22:20–21)

> When a stranger resides with you in your land, you shall not wrong him. The stranger who resides with you shall be to you as one of your citizens; you shall love him as yourself, for you

were strangers in the land of Egypt: I Adonai am your God.
(Leviticus 19:33–34)

You shall not subvert the rights of the stranger or the fatherless;
you shall not take a widow's garment in pawn. Remember
that you were a slave in Egypt and that Adonai your God
redeemed you from there; therefore do I enjoin you to
observe this commandment. (Deuteronomy 24:17–18)

For two millennia, Western philosophy has strived to establish
a basis for ethics beyond the power of external authority. Plato
retells the famous Myth of Gyges—the magical ring that rendered
its bearer invisible. Absent the fear of punishment, he wonders,
why would anyone be good? Why would anyone do the right
thing? Philosophers have argued that ethics are an expression of
our nature as rational beings. Others have maintained that ethics
express our duty to universal maxims. Still others have held that
ethics are a necessary condition for civil society, a social contract
upheld by civilized people. The Torah has a different basis for ethics. Ethics may be informed by rationality, intuition, conscience,
and social norms. But ethics begin much deeper, in the reflex of
perception. Do we see the other? Do we acknowledge the humanity of the other?

Sight is a reflex triggered by light striking the eye and send-
ing an impulse through the optic nerve to the brain. But vision is
much more complicated. Vision is conditioned by culture, by personality, by expectation. Vision is not passive. We see what we are
trained to see. We overlook what we are taught to ignore. We perceive through screens erected by our culture. It was expected that
a black woman would give up her seat on the bus to a white man
in 1954 Montgomery, Alabama. It was normal. No one noticed
until Rosa Parks refused. When I was young, boys could dream of
becoming astronauts, firemen, scientists. Girls were offered three

choices: teacher, nurse, or mommy. Women went to college to obtain a "Mrs. degree." No one noticed until Betty Friedan made us see. Every culture labels certain social facts as inevitable and "normal" and relegates them to invisibility. Every culture relegates certain people or classes of people to invisibility.

In Egypt, we experienced the condition of ultimate social invisibility. Unseen, unvalued, inconsequential, the slave is socially erased. We remember the humiliation and pain of that experience. From that experience grew the Torah's imperative that no human being ever be relegated to invisibility. Egyptian slavery taught us to see the other. Egypt taught us to see ourselves in the other, to identify with the pain and plight of the other. It taught that indifference to the suffering of the other is a denial of the self. The tightly drawn circle of the ego is pried open to include an other with whom we are one. For the Torah, ethics are based on empathy. And empathy is rooted in memory. Each year, we revisit Egypt to renew those memories and the acute sensitivity it engenders. That sensitivity defines Jewish ethics. It equips us to become vessels of divine blessing on earth.

Note the one small detail from the mitzvah in Deuteronomy: "You shall not take a widow's garment in pawn." Who is she? This woman who stands silently on the street corner—once she was a woman of means, with a life filled with promise. And then a catastrophe—a disease, a business failure, a crime, and she is left bereft, with children to feed. So what does she do? She sells her possessions to support the children—the furniture, the jewelry, the clothes. And when she exhausts all that, what is left? She sells her last garment, she offers up her dignity, her humanity— she sells herself. "See her!" demands the Torah. "Don't avert your eyes!" You know her humiliation; you too were once on society's periphery, neglected and abused. You must never allow a human being to fall to those depths.

Egypt taught us more than a personal ethic. Egypt taught us a
social philosophy. Civilizations are measured by the power of their
armies, the prosperity of their economies, the grandeur of their
cities. That's not the Torah's standard. Torah judges a civilization
based on its responsibility to the most vulnerable. The poor, bereft
woman who must sell her dignity on the street is a more significant
test of a society than the monuments that line its boulevards. Egypt
is renown for its monuments. But looking up at those monuments
from the vantage of the slave yields a very different perspective. So
the prophet Amos proclaimed:

Thus said Adonai:
> For three transgressions of Israel,
> For four, I will not revoke it:
> Because they have sold for silver
> Those whose cause was just,
> And the needy for a pair of sandals.
> [Ah,] you who trample the heads of the poor
> Into the dust of the ground,
> And make the humble walk a twisted course!
> Father and son go to the same girl,
> And thereby profane My holy name.
> They recline by every altar
> On garments taken in pledge,
> And drink in the House of their God
> Wine bought with fines they imposed....
> Hear this word, O people of Israel,
> That Adonai has spoken concerning you,
> Concerning the whole family that I brought up
>   from the land of Egypt:
> You alone have I singled out
> Of all the families of the earth—

That is why I will call you to account
For all your iniquities.
(Amos 2:6–8, 3:1–2)

Every mitzvah is one step on the path from Egypt to Eden. But with all the failures of human character, what gives us the resolve to continue the journey? What gives us any confidence that we might ever arrive? Every week, we are given a glimpse down the road. Every week, we are granted a taste of Eden.

SHABBAT: A TASTE OF EDEN

Observe the Sabbath day and keep it holy, as Adonai your God has commanded you. Six days you shall labor and do all your work, but the seventh day is a Sabbath of Adonai your God; you shall not do any work—you, your son or your daughter, your male or female slave, your ox or your ass, or any of your cattle, or the stranger in your settlements, so that your male and female slave may rest as you do. Remember that you were a slave in the land of Egypt and Adonai your God freed you from there with a mighty hand and an outstretched arm; therefore Adonai your God has commanded you to observe the Sabbath day. (Deuteronomy 5:12–15)

On Shabbat, everyone rests—the householder, the family, the servants, the slaves, even the animals, even God. No one serves another. On Shabbat, all become equal. On Shabbat, the social hierarchy collapses. We become one—one with one another, one with all other living things, one with God. That's Eden. Six days a week, we toil in a world that is all too much like Egypt. But for twenty-five hours each week, we are given a free pass to visit the Garden and enjoy its serenity and unity. Once a week, we are offered a chance to step out of the world's brokenness to experience a world perfected. We know that our aspiration is not unreachable, because we visit it every week. We continue the journey toward Eden because each week we are given a taste of its sweetness.

Halfway between Egypt and Eden rises Mount Sinai. At Sinai, the people Israel are given the map of the route of their moral journey, a picture of the landscape they must traverse, and a vision of its goal, the Promised Land.

KEDUSHAH: A VISION OF THE PROMISED LAND

> *Kedoshim tihyu, ki kadosh ani Adonai Eloheicheim.* You shall be
> holy, for I, Adonai your God, am holy. (Leviticus 19:2)

Kedushah, translated as "holiness," is the highest spiritual virtue in Judaism. According to the Torah, it is the singular quality of God that we are to imitate. For all of God's infinity, this quality of God lies within our potential. In this one quality, we can be like God, we can be Godly.

But what is it? What is *kedushah*?

The conventional definition of *kedushah*, "holiness," has to do with separateness—that which is set apart for special purposes. That which is holy is restricted. The Sabbath is set aside from the days of the week. Israel is set apart from the nations of the world.

But there is another way to look at the very same phenomena—the obverse of the same definition. Look at how the word *kedushah* is used in Jewish life.

Gathered around a table, on Shabbat or a holiday, we stand as a circle of family or friends, and we raise a cup of wine and recite a blessing. It isn't the wine that is blessed. It is the moment of intimacy, of sharing, of oneness. That prayer is called *Kiddush*.

Two loving friends pledge to share life together, to share laughter and tears, to share dreams and disappointments. A ring is placed on the right forefinger and a promise is uttered: *Harei at mikudeshet li.* You are mine, soul mate, lover, friend. Marriage in Hebrew is called *kiddushin.*

When a loved one dies, we come to realize that love never dies. We never let go. They live with us—their wisdom, their love, their kindness, their influence. So we stand up in the presence of community and recite a prayer, a declaration of loyalty, and that's called *Kaddish.*

Kiddush, kiddushin, Kaddish, kadosh, kedushah, all mean "holiness," and all mean opening the self to embrace another, bonding with another, holding the other close, never letting go, making the other part of the self. We form around ourselves a circle, a circle of our intimate concern, the people we care for, the ones we define as ours. For some, the circumference of that circle is so narrow, it includes only the individual self, its diameter reaching only to the end of the nose. For others, the circle includes family, community, nation. For a very few, it encompasses the whole of the world. We worship a God whose circle of concern is infinite. *Adonai Echad,* "Adonai is One"—God is the infinite circle of concern that embraces all of life. The aspiration to *kedushah* is rooted in the conviction that the wider our circle of concern, the more godly our life. The wider the circle of responsibility, the more meaningful, the deeper, is life. Each step we take to open the circle and include another brings God into our life.

What is the opposite of holiness? At the end of Shabbat, we recite a blessing on the distinction between the holy and the ordinary—*hamavdil bein kodesh lechol.* The Hebrew word for the opposite of holy—for the profane, the mundane, the ordinary—is *hol,* which literally means "sand." Try to hold a handful of sand; what happens? Atomized, individuated, disconnected, unbound, the grains slip away. That's the opposite of holiness.

Remembering the slavery of Egypt forms the moral minimum for a Jew. *Kedoshim tihyu,* "you will be holy," points to the moral ideal—the goal of our long journey. Each gesture of bonding brings to reality a bit of the divine dream, a world made whole, a world made holy, a world returned to the ideal of Eden. We acknowledge this in the blessing recited upon the performance of each gesture:

Baruch atah Adonai,
Eloheinu Melech ha-olam,
asher kideshanu be-mitzvotav ...
Praised are You, Adonai, our God,
whose presence fills the universe,
who brings us kedushah, oneness, with this mitzvah,
this gesture of holiness.

Just a few verses after *Kedoshim tihyu* in Leviticus is the highest moral ideal: *Ve-ahavta le-rei'acha kamocha*, "You will love your neighbor as yourself" (Leviticus 19:18). This is our ideal—the oneness of Eden. We are one. We come to realize a self that includes the other. Love the other who is your self, whose suffering is yours and whose destiny you share. Every human transaction, teaches the Torah, must lead us to the realization of a world in which we are one, bound together.

The narrative arc of the Torah brings us from the divine dream of the Garden, through the torturous oppression of Egyptian slavery, and onto the road toward Eden. But this time, Eden will not be given to us as God's gift. This Eden will be constructed and maintained by human hands. That's the purpose of Torah. And that is the eternal mission of the Jewish people—to replant the Garden, with its oneness and its peace. That is chutzpah at its highest.

Chapter Three

JEWS GONE WILD

Once a year, Jews go wild. Once a year, all the normal habits of Jewish life are meticulously overturned. The religious tradition that customarily counsels sober reflection directs Jews to indulge in inebriation until all moral distinctions are erased. The synagogue, usually a place where truth is revealed and revered, is filled with Jews hiding behind masks and costumes. A book of scripture is read publicly, but with none of the reverence reserved for holy texts. Instead, the reading is met with noisemakers, hoots, hollers, and cheers. On Purim, Jews go wild.

Purim celebrates the redemption of the Jews of Persia as told in the biblical book of Esther. It is the Jewish edition of Mardi Gras, our "feast of fools," when the discipline of the synagogue is loosened to admit uncontained revelry and uncompromised joy. But there is something sacred in Purim's madness. The Talmud teaches that in the time of the Messiah, no holidays will be celebrated except Purim, and no other books of the Bible will be preserved except the five books of Torah and the book of Esther.[1] Why Esther? Why Purim?

The word *purim* is Persian for "casting lots" or "throwing the dice." *Purim* means "chance." Genesis portrays a cosmos ordered by a beneficent Creator. Exodus celebrates the purposeful journey of history. Esther offers the opposite—a world of randomness, accident, and chance. Esther poses a serious challenge to the Bible.

Chutzpah, the Jewish vision of human possibility, fits well into the ordered world of Genesis and Exodus. Where does chutzpah fit into a world that is arbitrary, haphazard, and cruel? What human possibilities can be celebrated in an irrational world, the world of power plays, gambits, and gambles?

The book of Esther is a drama of four archetypal characters: the king, Ahasuerus; the villain, Haman; the hero, Mordecai; and the princess, Esther.

ENTER THE KING

> It happened in the days of Ahasuerus—that Ahasuerus who reigned over a hundred and twenty-seven provinces from India to Nubia. In those days, when King Ahasuerus occupied the royal throne in the fortress Shushan, in the third year of his reign, he gave a banquet for all the officials and courtiers....
> (Esther 1:1–3)

Welcome to Shushan. The Torah offers us a world governed by a just and moral God. But Shushan isn't ruled by God. Shushan is ruled by Ahasuerus, the king of chaos. Ahasuerus is a fool, motivated only by his immediate pleasure and whim. He is a ruler without rules. He has neither wisdom nor conscience nor foresight. When circumstances demand that he govern, he waits for someone to tell him what to do. He is oblivious to the consequences of his decisions, which inevitably spin far out of his control.

Ahasuerus is power.

The book of Esther is easily the funniest book in the Hebrew Bible. It is also deadly serious. Esther is a political parable disguised as a ribald satire on Persian court life. It is a dizzying read, veering sharply between chapters of ridiculous farce and chapters that coldly detail the machinations of genocidal evil. Esther is beloved for its silliness. But the silliness masks an earnest warning to those who live in a world without order. Behind the mask of hilarity, Esther is a handbook of Jewish survival in the Diaspora, a guide to those who aspire to do good in an amoral world, and a meditation on human possibilities in a chaotic world.

Lesson number one: Power is blind and witless. Power has no plan, no vision, no values. Power invites manipulation. In our world, no one is in charge. No one is driving. Power in this world is a foolish drunk—clueless, careless, indifferent, and blind.

The opening scene of the book of Esther offers a delicious glimpse into the zany life of the royal court. Ahasuerus celebrates his dominion with a six-month-long World's Fair culminating in a seven-day wine feast. At the height of the party, when the king is good and drunk, he orders his prize wife Vashti to appear before the court "to display her beauty to the peoples and the officials; for she was a beautiful woman" (Esther 1:11). In the world's first recorded feminist protest, Vashti refuses to be displayed. Ahasuerus is incensed. But he hasn't a clue what to do. Ahasuerus rules an empire, but he is stymied by a willful woman. It is the court eunuch, ironically the only real man in attendance, who points out that Vashti's refusal is not just a personal affront to the king but also a subversion of civil and natural order:

> "Queen Vashti has committed an offense not only against Your Majesty but also against all the officials and against all the men in all the provinces of King Ahasuerus. For the queen's behavior will make all wives disregard their husbands, ... and there will be no end of disrespect and provocation!" (Esther 1:16–18)

Catastrophe is averted with Vashti's exile. Which leaves the king without a consort. Which leads to the conscription of every young unmarried woman in the empire into the king's harem. Which will bring Esther, the daughter of Jewish exiles, into the king's inner chamber. Politics in this world is a comedy of errors, a ballet of clowns and buffoons. And this would be hilarious, except when it turns deadly.

ENTER HAMAN

> Some time afterward, King Ahasuerus promoted Haman, son of Hammedatha the Agagite; he advanced him and seated him higher than any of his fellow officials. All the king's courtiers in the palace gate knelt and bowed low to Haman, for such was the king's order concerning him; but Mordecai would not kneel or bow low. Then the king's courtiers who were in the palace gate said to Mordecai, "Why do you disobey the king's order?" When they spoke to him day after day and he would not listen to them, they told Haman, in order to see whether Mordecai's resolve would prevail; for he had explained to them that he was a Jew. (Esther 3:1–4)

Haman is identified as an Agagite, a descendant of the ancient king of Amalek, the perennial enemy of the Jewish people. He receives obeisance from all, except Mordecai the Jew. Why Mordecai refuses to bow to Haman is not made clear. Was his refusal a religious gesture, refusing to bow to any but God? Was it a reflection of Haman's hateful patrimony? Was it a personal rivalry? In any case, Mordecai's refusal becomes Haman's obsession. Just like Ahasuerus's preoccupation with Vashti, Haman, who now rules nations and empires, is fixated on this one man's intransigence. But unlike the befuddled king, Haman knows exactly what to do.

> When Haman saw that Mordecai would not kneel or bow low to him, Haman was filled with rage. But he disdained to lay hands on Mordecai alone; having been told who Mordecai's people were, Haman plotted to do away with all the Jews, Mordecai's people, throughout the kingdom of Ahasuerus. (Esther 3:5–6)

Haman is evil. Evil is the worship of the self above all else, the insatiable drive to aggrandize the self. Evil is ready to destroy anything that casts a shadow over the self. Because the Jewish people have always been the outlier—the visible exception to someone's dream of universal dominion and uniformity of opinion—they have been evil's most enduring victim. Throughout history, the presence of the Jew always compromised someone's fantasy of ubiquitous authority. Haman was only the first to be irritated by a Jew's presumptuous refusal to bow low. But the Jew, as it has been said, is only the canary in the mine. The Jew represents all who would stand in the face of authority and demand a place, a voice, a vote for those who are different. And the Hamans of the world always react the same way. For evil to prevail, it must find its way to power. Haman approaches Ahasuerus with his plan. Into his mouth, the book of Esther puts the historically classic soliloquy of hate.

> Haman then said to King Ahasuerus, "There is a certain people, scattered and dispersed among the other peoples in all the provinces of your realm, whose laws are different from those of any other people and who do not obey the king's laws; and it is not in Your Majesty's interest to tolerate them. If it please Your Majesty, let an edict be drawn for their destruction, and I will pay ten thousand talents of silver to the stewards for deposit in the royal treasury." Thereupon the king removed his signet ring from his hand and gave it to Haman, son of Hammedatha the Agagite, the foe of the Jews. And the king said, "The money and the people are yours to do with as you see fit." (Esther 3:8–11)

In the ancient world, the leaders of a conquered people would be exiled to the imperial capital. Defeated militarily and separated from their native land, language, and culture, they would soon assimilate into the majority culture. But "there is a certain people," these Jews, who somehow manage to maintain their cultural identity in exile. This people, warns Haman, look like us, dress like us, talk like us, but they aren't like us. They are unnatural and uncanny, and they are dangerous, they are a threat. The steps to genocide are all here: identify the other; castigate the other; dehumanize the other; destroy the other. Haman sets the formula for the generations of hatred and murder that will succeed him.

And Ahasuerus, who deliberated mightily on the fate of his defiant wife, Vashti, here instantly and idly removes his ring and condemns all of Persia's Jews to death. Power is blind and foolish. Evil only needs momentary access to power to achieve untold destruction.

> On the thirteenth day of the first month, the king's scribes were summoned and a decree was issued, as Haman directed.... Written instructions were dispatched by couriers to all the king's provinces to destroy, massacre, and exterminate all the Jews, young and old, children and women, on a single day, on the thirteenth day of the twelfth month—that is, the month of Adar—and to plunder their possessions.... The king and Haman sat down to feast, but the city of Shushan was dumbfounded. (Esther 3:12–13, 3:15)

How do we survive in such a world? What chance has good against evil so devious?

ENTER THE HERO

> In the fortress Shushan lived a Jew by the name of Mordecai, son of Jair son of Shimei son of Kish, a Benjaminite. [Kish] had been exiled from Jerusalem in the group that was carried into exile along with King Jeconiah of Judah, which had been driven into exile by King Nebuchadnezzar of Babylon. (Esther 2:5–6)

The name "Mordecai" is derived from "Marduk," the patron god of the Babylonian Empire. When does a subjugated people name its children for the god of the nation that conquered them? When they have assimilated. Mordecai is the name of conscientious citizenship—the good man, the good citizen, the good Diaspora Jew—respected, respectful, and utterly conventional. He is a man of prominence in Shushan, a loyal and productive citizen of his new native land. In one episode, he foils a plot to assassinate Ahasuerus and is rewarded royally. With all that, Mordecai is not entirely at ease. When his orphaned niece, Esther, is conscripted into the king's harem, along with all the other young women of the land, he warns her not to reveal her identity. Deep within, the eternal strain of Jewish nervousness still rules Mordecai's heart. And soon enough, this very ancient fear comes roaring to life.

> When Mordecai learned all that had happened, Mordecai tore his clothes and put on sackcloth and ashes.... Also, in every province that the king's command and decree reached, there was great mourning among the Jews, with fasting, weeping, and wailing, and everybody lay in sackcloth and ashes. (Esther 4:1, 4:3)

In the Torah, obedience to God brings reward. Disobedience brings punishment. If catastrophe threatens, it is surely punishment for some sin, and therefore cause for prayer and repentance. The gestures of mourning—sackcloth and ashes—denote humility in the face of the punishing God. Mordecai leads the community in these traditional rituals—fasting, praying, mourning. But to no avail. No miracles ensue, no plagues fall on our enemies, no Moses arrives to save the Jews. In fact, nothing Mordecai does is effective—neither his stature and standing as good citizen, nor his reputation as the king's rescuer, nor his religiosity. And none of the traditional responses to communal danger elicit a response.

Mordecai fails. In this chaotic, amoral world, a world ruled by random chance, the conventional strategies of survival fail.

Lesson number two: Evil will always finds its way to power unless the good are sufficiently aggressive and resourceful to stop it. In this world, all the conventional strategies—loyalty to the state, attentive observance of civic duties, conscientious practice of virtue—fail to hold back evil's progress. Even religious devotion fails.

How can that be? The Torah assured us that the universe is governed by a moral and just God, a God who will rescue God's people from adversity. Where is that God in Shushan?

Find a child who watches Disney movies, and ask the child to name this story: It takes place somewhere in the Middle East. It features four characters—a foolish king, his evil advisor, a beautiful princess, and a brave hero. Any kid will tell you, that's *Aladdin*. In *Aladdin* we have a silly king, the evil Jafar, the beautiful Princess Jasmine, and Aladdin the hero. In Esther, we have Ahasuerus the king, evil Haman, beautiful Esther, and loyal Mordecai. Same characters, same story. Esther and Aladdin are both derived from the long folklore tradition of Persian court dramas. The story and its characters are familiar, with one notable exception. In an egregious departure from the literary genre, an important character is missing from Esther—the genie. Aladdin was saved by the genie in the lamp who granted his wishes. In the Disney version, the genie is brilliantly voiced by the actor Robin Williams. There should be a genie in Esther who saves the day, and it is clear who should play this role. God should be our genie! Mordecai should rub a lamp, and God should emerge to save the Jews of Persia! But God refuses to enter this story. Nowhere in the book of Esther is God's name mentioned. Nowhere is God visibly present.

Lesson number three: God is not your genie. If you and your ideals are to survive in this morally chaotic world, you must find the power somewhere else. God may be present in the world of Shushan, but not as in Exodus, not as a visible, redeeming power, splitting seas and destroying our enemies. In what way is God present?

ENTER ESTHER

[Mordecai] was foster father to Hadassah—that is, Esther—his uncle's daughter, for she had neither father nor mother. The maiden was shapely and beautiful; and when her father and mother died, Mordecai adopted her as his own daughter.

When the king's order and edict was proclaimed, and when many girls were assembled in the fortress Shushan under the supervision of Hegai, Esther too was taken into the king's palace.... Esther won the admiration of all who saw her.

Esther was taken to King Ahasuerus.... The king loved Esther more than all the other women, and she won his grace and favor more than all the virgins. So he set a royal diadem on her head and made her queen instead of Vashti. (Esther 2:7–8, 2:15–17)

Like Mordecai, Esther bears the name of a foreign god, Ishtar, the Mesopotamian goddess of fertility, love, and war. In Mesopotamian mythology, Ishtar descends into the underworld—the Land of No Return—to rescue her lover, Tammuz. Ishtar must shed a piece of her clothing to pass each of the underworld's seven gates, until she stands naked before the jealous Queen of the Underworld, who incarcerates her, inflicting upon her sixty miseries. With Ishtar imprisoned, the world's fertility ceases; death rules and no new life is created. This spurs Ea, the king of the gods, to rescue her and return life to the world.

The journey of Ishtar is the backdrop to the drama of Queen Esther. Entering the palace, Esther enters her own Land of No

Return. One by one, she gives up the elements of her identity. Her name, her people, her family, her values, her history are lost to her. All contact with the world is lost. When her uncle Mordecai comes to inform her of Haman's genocidal decree, a reality unknown to her, she is upset, not by the tragic news of immanent destruction, but by Mordecai's odd demeanor. The real prospect of her people's demise brings her no grief. But the disheveled ranting man at the palace gates is a threat.

> When Esther's maidens and eunuchs came and informed her, the queen was greatly agitated. She sent clothing for Mordecai to wear, so that he might take off his sackcloth; but he refused. (Esther 4:4)

Having exhausted all other means to stop the destruction of Persia's Jews, Mordecai must turn to Esther for help. He details Haman's plan. But Esther's resistance only stiffens. She wants nothing to do with this. Life in the palace is good; why should she worry herself about the events in a world now far away? She responds to Mordecai's pleas with a precise citation of palace protocol:

> "All the king's courtiers and the people of the king's provinces know that if any person, man or woman, enters the king's presence in the inner court without having been summoned, there is but one law for him—that he be put to death. Only if the king extends the golden scepter to him may he live. Now I have not been summoned to visit the king for the last thirty days." (Esther 4:11)

Esther is trapped in the Land of No Return. The shocking dissymmetry between Mordecai's plea for the life of their people and Esther's autonomic palace-speak reveals how lost she has become. To save his people, Mordecai realizes he must first save his niece. He must revive her conscience and recover her identity.

> When Mordecai was told what Esther had said, Mordecai had
> this message delivered to Esther: "Do not imagine that you, of
> all the Jews, will escape with your life by being in the king's
> palace. On the contrary, if you keep silent in this crisis, relief
> and deliverance will come to the Jews from another quar-
> ter, while you and your father's house will perish. And who
> knows, perhaps you have attained to royal position for just
> such a crisis." (Esther 4:12–14)

We can feel Mordecai's urgency. Like her namesake, Ishtar, all of
life depends on Esther, on Mordecai's ability to retrieve and revive
Esther. How do you awaken a sleeping soul? How do you make
someone care? He begins with the pragmatic and moves to the
lofty, from the personal to the metaphysical.

Your fate is inevitably and indelibly tied to our fate, he tells
her. You won't "pass" forever. When they come for us, they will
come for you too. But know this: If you hide, indifferent to our
shared fate, you will bring death to whatever in you remains
authentic and real. If you stand by, oblivious to this, all that
defines you will be erased. You will become Vashti, just another
of Ahasuerus's trophies, an ornament.

Finally, he begs her to reflect on her purpose. Why are you
here? How did you get here? See: you are part of something bigger, a grander narrative, a greater drama. But he does not evoke
God. There is no voice from out of a burning bush. Instead, he
evokes chutzpah. You are here for a purpose, he assures her, a
task that only you can accomplish. This task claims you. It is
the source of your significance. The world may be governed by
chance, but if we rise to our responsibilities and act, chaos is not
inevitable. You must interpose yourself between evil and power.
And only you, who is intimate with power, can do this. This is
your moment.

Something within Esther wakes up. Suddenly, she sees herself and her circumstance. She accepts the responsibility.

> Then Esther sent back this answer to Mordecai: "Go, assemble all the Jews who live in Shushan, and fast in my behalf; do not eat or drink for three days, night or day. I and my maidens will observe the same fast. Then I shall go to the king, though it is contrary to the law; and if I am to perish, I shall perish!" (Esther 4:15–16)

Contrary to her fears, Esther is welcomed by the king. She invites him and Haman to a wine feast and then another. And when the moment is ripe, she springs her trap.

> On the second day, the king again asked Esther at the wine feast, "What is your wish, Queen Esther? It shall be granted you. And what is your request? Even to half the kingdom, it shall be fulfilled." Queen Esther replied: "If Your Majesty will do me the favor, and if it pleases Your Majesty, let my life be granted me as my wish, and my people as my request. For we have been sold, my people and I, to be destroyed, massacred, and exterminated...." Thereupon King Ahasuerus demanded of Queen Esther, "Who is he and where is he who dared to do this?" "The adversary and enemy," replied Esther, "is this evil Haman!" (Esther 7:2–6)

And so, the wheel of fortune turns. All that Haman planned for Mordecai is instead done to Haman. Mordecai is elevated to the king's right hand. The Jews defend themselves against the decree and win a great battle. A joyous holiday is established, celebrated year to year with feasting, neighborly generosity, and laughter.

Lesson number four: Evil always strives to find its way to power. The only way for good to triumph is to prevent evil from connecting with power. But this cannot be accomplished from outside the circles of power. No matter how much goodness might benefit the realm, good remains impotent standing outside the palace, outside power's proximity. The only way to keep evil from power is to get closer to power than does evil—to woo power, to seduce power, to sleep with power. The good may find this distasteful. After all, goodness should be self-evident, as the destructive consequences of embracing evil are self-evident. But that's not how things work in the world of Shushan. Ahasuerus is a blind, drunk fool. In his kingdom, neither good nor evil has preeminence. Whoever gets to power first, whoever stays closest to power, prevails. That's the only way.

But there is a paradox. Like the myth of Ishtar, access to power is granted only those willing to strip off all that clothes them, all that protects and identifies them. The closer one draws toward power, the less of yourself do you bring with you. Coming close to power, one can easily forget one's history, identity, values. The closer you come to power, the harder it is to remember why you sought power in the first place, why you are there. Soon, being with power is all that matters. Ahasuerus's presence renders everyone drunk. It takes a miracle to awaken a soul to the larger purposes power might serve, to the dangers of evil, to the possibilities of good. It takes a miracle to believe that one can yet change the course of history, that what is, is not what inevitably must be. It takes a miracle to summon the courage to move the world, with all its randomness, toward right. That is the miracle of Esther. Where is God in the insane world of Shushan? In Esther. In her newly wakened sense of responsibility, in her renewed sense of her own possibilities, in her courage. In her chutzpah.

Once a year, we Jews go wild. We turn the synagogue into Shushan. With noisemakers and masks, with drinking and laughter, we conscientiously overturn all our rules and traditions. Why do Jews go wild once a year? Because we are not afraid of the chaos.

We can laugh at it because we know what can be accomplished by dedicated human beings even in the world of random chance and chaos. We believe in the power of chutzpah, and so we can join Ahasuerus's feast and celebrate.

Chapter Four

THE WORLD STANDS ON THREE PILLARS

It was the most beautiful building in the ancient world. The Temple of Jerusalem was a cube of gleaming, immaculate white marble crowned with a golden parapet that ran along the roofline. The wide courtyard was ringed in three rows of white marble columns and paved in white marble. Set within the Judean hills, the gleam of the marble and gold could be seen from miles away. Jewish pilgrims came from across the Mediterranean to worship in its precincts. Tourists and travelers of every nation came to Jerusalem to behold the Temple's magnificent beauty and to witness its majestic rites.

Constructed originally by King Solomon in 970 BCE, sacked by the Assyrians in the eighth century BCE, destroyed by the Babylonians in 586 BCE, rebuilt by Ezra and Nehemiah a generation later, and finally made resplendent by King Herod under the Roman Empire, the Temple had stood on its sacred foundation for more than a millennium. For Jews, the Temple was the center of life; home to their collective civic life, cultural life, education, commerce, and government. The Temple was that unique and holy place where heaven and earth touched; its rites gave tangible evidence of God's loving presence in the life of the Jewish people. The community's collective and personal emotional life was expressed through its rituals—thanksgiving, expiation of sin, release from guilt, the collective expression of hope and national dreams. Most importantly for the ancient Jew, God lived in the Temple. Deep within the Temple was a special room, the *Kodesh Ha-Kodashim*, the Holy of Holies, the inner sanctum. In Solomon's Temple, that room held the Ark of the Covenant, constructed by Moses in the desert. In the Second Temple, following the Babylonian exile, the room was empty. But every Jew believed that it contained the mysterious presence of the Divine. In that room resided an aspect of God's infinite power. Only one person ever entered that room—the High Priest, and only on the holiest day of the year, Yom Kippur. Having spent a month in meditation and preparation, the High Priest entered the holy place to beg forgiveness for the priesthood and the Levites and to ask blessings for his people. So fearsome was the experience, a rope was tied around him, so that if he died in the middle of the rite, his body could be dragged safely from the sacred room.

In the summer of the year 70 CE, it all came to an end. The Judeans launched a revolt. Rome, fearing the loss of its eastern borderland, responded decisively. The Romans landed the Tenth Legion, the mightiest of their armies, at Phoenicia, under the command of the revered general Vespesian, and marched down the coast, brutally destroying the towns, farms, and homesteads along the way. The Romans reached Jerusalem and laid siege to the holy city. On the seventeenth of the month of Tammuz, the walls of Jerusalem were breached, and three weeks later, on the ninth of Av, the Temple was destroyed. As a demonstration of imperial power, the Romans razed the entire city, pulled down its walls, burned its homes, upturned the paving of its streets, and smashed its marketplaces.

For the Jews who survived, the Temple's destruction was beyond catastrophic. The Temple represented their identity, their

place in the world, and their relationship to God. It was all suddenly
lost. Everything that tied Jews to their history, their culture, their
faith, everything that held the community together, was destroyed.
The Temple was built upon *even hashtiyah*, the mythical foundation stone of the world—*axis mundi*, the world's keystone. When
the Temple was destroyed, it appeared that great stone was also
destroyed, so that for the Jews of the first century, the destruction of the Temple literally knocked the world off its foundation,
off its axis. To this day, wherever they are in the world, Jews have
turned toward the Temple site to pray. Typically, that is eastward,
so the Temple provided the Jews with literal and spiritual "ori-
entation." Losing the Temple brought severe "disorientation" for
Jews everywhere.

The people Israel desperately sought some way to understand
and respond to the catastrophe. The nascent Christian community had a ready explanation. The Jews, they explained, had cal-
lously rejected God's Messiah, and this was the punishment. The
Romans had their explanation: the victory of the Roman armies
was proof of the superiority of the Roman gods and the impotence
of the Jewish God. After all, they asked derisively, what sort of god
would allow that god's city and temple to be destroyed and the
people to be humiliated? And no doubt, there were certainly numbers of Jews who responded to these interpretations.

Those who sought some Jewish understanding came before
the only surviving teacher of Judaism—Rabbi Yochanan ben
Zakkai. In the midst of the failed rebellion, Rabbi Yochanan made
a separate peace with the Roman authorities and was permitted
to establish an academy near the town of Yavneh. There is no historical record of his conversation with the refugees, but it takes
just a little imagination for those of us born in the shadow of the
twentieth century's Holocaust to hear the questions they asked.
The survivors likely came to Rabbi Yochanan and asked the great

questions of every post-Holocaust Judaism: We have no home in the world. We have no Temple, no priests, no sacrifices. What do we do? How do we go on? Where do we belong? What does this mean for our national existence? What is our collective purpose now? They likely asked, Why did this happen? Most painfully, they surely asked, Does God hate us? Has God abandoned us? Is the Jewish people finished? Why should we go on living as Jews?

And it takes but little imagination to grasp the existential decision facing Rabbi Yochanan. What hope could he offer his people? Should he promise that God would soon rescue them with signs and wonders as in Egypt? Or was the Temple's destruction in fact the empirical proof that the Jewish people's time had come to an end? Was it time to surrender? He chose another answer, an answer that is the very height of chutzpah.

A NEW HOME FOR GOD IN THE WORLD

There is no historical record of the conversation, only of its consequences. And from them we can surmise what Rabbi Yochanan said. In the subsequent generations, Rabbi Yochanan's successors will create the vast literature of Jewish wisdom we call Talmud. Among the volumes of the Talmud, there is one unique book, *Pirke Avot* (the Wisdom of the Sages). *Pirke Avot* contains the responses of Rabbi Yochanan and his students to the spiritual devastation of their generation. It is a handbook for recreating Jewish life in the face of catastrophe; the instruction manual for a post-Holocaust Judaism. Responding to the crisis, Rabbi Yochanan quoted the teaching of his ancestor, Shimon Ha-Zaddik, a teaching his students would include in the very first chapter of *Pirke Avot*:

> *The world stands*
> *On three things,*
> *On Torah, on worship, on acts of kindness.*[1]

Your world stands, he assured them. What you have lost is a building, a city, a state, but the world that is your home has not perished. Home is not a physical place, a location, a building, or a piece of real estate. Home is not an accident of geography. It is an illusion to think that a building, a plot of ground, or the political or military control over a piece of land will give you the security of being at home—the assurance of belonging in the world, a sense of place and of peace. We have lost a physical Temple. Now we will set about rebuilding the Jewish world on surer spiritual grounds.

God's presence is accessible to you, taught Rabbi Yochanan, but no longer through the sacrificial rites of the Temple, and no longer mediated by priests. God is present to you in the Torah you learn, in the worship you offer, and in the acts of kindness you perform in the world. God's presence is no longer contained in a room, in a building, on a hill in Jerusalem. God's presence in the world is now your responsibility. God's presence is mediated by your actions and devotion.

God has no geography. These gestures of learning, worship, and kindness can be performed anywhere. For Yochanan ben Zakkai, the destruction of the Temple did not banish God from the world. On the contrary, it liberated God from the narrow confines of the Holy of Holies into the whole of the world. It released the worship of God from the authority of the priesthood into the hands of common Jews. It opened a door to the development of new institutions of Jewish life. Ironically, the destruction, as devastating as it appeared, assured the continuance of Jewish life into the next millennium.

The heart of our renewed Jewish devotion is study of Torah; therefore the school, or *beit midrash,* is the new heart of the Jewish community. In practice, there is no institution in Jewish life that mirrors what we call "school." School, in American parlance, is a place for children. A *beit midrash* is always filled with adults. In America, we educate children to enter adulthood. They look forward to "graduating" from school to enter life. By contrast, in Jewish life, education is a lifelong occupation. One never graduates. Rather, the goal of Jewish devotion is to be counted as a *talmid chacham*—a perpetual student of wisdom. One does not learn in order to make a living, as we do in American culture. Rather, in Jewish tradition, one strives to make a living in order to afford the opportunity to learn. "If I were a rich man," dreamed Tevye in *Fiddler on the Roof,* "I'd sit and study the holy books seven hours every day ... that would be the sweetest thing of all!"

When the Temple was destroyed, animal sacrifice ceased. So Jews elevated verbal prayer as their idiom of expression before God. And verbal prayer is celebrated in the synagogue, or *beit kenesset.* Sacrifice was a disciplined expression of communal devotion, so the rabbis of Yavneh set about to create the first Jewish prayer book—a standardized collection of common prayer, so that to this day, a Jew in any community in the world can join a *minyan*, a service, and share the communal devotion of Jewish prayer.

Beit midrash is the locus of Torah, and *beit kenesset* is the locus of prayer. What is the place devoted to the practice of kindness? The Jewish home. The Bible does not contain a philosophy of home life. Its concern is principally with national life. The Rabbis of Yavneh constructed an ideology of the Jewish home, elevating domesticity to sanctity. As a symbol of this, they brought rituals of the Temple worship into the home. On Friday night, for example, before we share the sweet challah, we wash our hands and recite the blessing *Al netilat yadayim.* Nowhere in the Torah is a common Jew commanded to wash before eating; rather, it was the priests who washed before eating holy offerings. And then after the blessing, it is customary to sprinkle salt on the challah. Why? Because every offering of the Temple was offered with salt. In fact, the word *challah* initially referred to the portion of bread dough that belonged to the priests. We all share the challah on Friday night, because in the Rabbis' vision, we now share the prerogatives of the priests. The family table becomes the altar, and the family home becomes the new Holy of Holies, the dwelling of God in the world. According to an opinion recorded in the Talmud, "At the time when the Temple stood, the altar made atonement for a person. Now, a person's table makes atonement for him."[2]

Yochanan ben Zakkai and his colleagues created a new home for God in the world. They rescued Judaism in its most perilous moment, choosing to continue in the face of the catastrophe of the Temple's destruction. To do so, they refashioned the practice of Judaism, removing it from a particular geography and political condition and resetting it upon new "pillars." They shaped a new organization of institutions to promulgate Jewish wisdom and Jewish life. Who gave them permission to do this?

TORAH AT THE CENTER

When we tell the story of Judaism, we typically tell a story of continuity—of a chain of tradition reaching back into antiquity. We gain a sense of authenticity from our faith that what we practice and believe is what our ancestors passed down to us—from Abraham, through Moses, to the prophets, the Rabbis, the sages, into our age. And we accept our sacred responsibility to pass this forward to our children and the generations to come. As a story of continuity, we are called upon not to be original or creative or inventive. We are called upon to transmit faithfully what we have received.

But there is another story of Judaism, a parallel story that is equally compelling. This is a story of Jewish discontinuity. At certain moments of history, conditions imposed from outside our community or development from within our community necessitated a radical rethinking of Jewish life. These moments demanded a reinterpretation of our core values and truths, a re-visioning of our collective mission, a reinvention of our central institutions and modes of expression. To assert the priority of tradition, of continuity, at these moments and resist the impulse to change would have terminated us as a people and a culture. Had Yochanan ben Zakkai told his generation to sit and wait for God's redemption, had he told them to anticipate an imminent return to Temple and priests and sacrifice, holding fast to the way things had always been, we would never have survived the catastrophe of destruction in 70 CE. Within a generation, Jewish life would have disappeared.

It takes a special courage to recognize that the moment demands something new. This is especially true for a culture that so reveres its past. It takes luminous creativity to conceive and shape and realize the new. And it takes deep wisdom to recognize what must change and what must remain unchanged. These qualities of leadership are the secret components of Jewish survival. At their common foundation lies the conviction that it is a human prerogative to set the terms of our covenant with God, and it is our responsibility to make a home for God in the world. This is the chutzpah of the Rabbis.

A conquered people, bereft of its Temple, exiled from its land, and removed from the symbols of its collective identity should have become dispirited and should have disappeared. That's certainly what the Romans were counting on. How did the Rabbis accomplish the resurrection of their people, the reconstitution of their religious culture, and the renewal of their national spirit and identity? How did they achieve this miracle?

In the book of Exodus, God commands, "Make for Me a sanctuary [*mikdash*] and I will dwell among them" (Exodus 25:8). In the wake of the brutal destruction of their Temple and homeland, the Rabbis came to understand that so long as God's sanctuary was a physical structure in the world, the people Israel would forever remain vulnerable to the accidents of history. They came to believe that the sanctuary's physical form was insignificant. What matters instead is the divine voice that rings from within it and the human solidarity that is achieved in the society constructed around it. So the Rabbis replaced the destroyed physical sanctuary (*mikdash*) with *midrash*—"study," the sanctuary of spiritual inquiry—and built their civilization on Torah.

Torah for the Rabbis was not solely the scroll kept in the synagogue, or the Five Books of Moses, or even the corpus of religious culture. For the Rabbis, Torah was the presence of God in the world. Torah replaced homeland, the soil out of which our collective life and identity grows. Torah replaced Temple, the meeting place of heaven and earth. Torah was the gateway to Eden, the eternal Jewish dream.

The visual focal point of every synagogue is the holy ark, *aron ha-kodesh*. This phrase hearkens back to the Ark of the Covenant created by Moses in the wilderness, the Ark that once rested in the Temple's inner sanctum, the *Kodesh Ha-Kodashim*, Holy of Holies. When God spoke with Moses in the wilderness, it was from the Ark. In the synagogue, God again speaks from the ark, only now the divine voice is communicated through the Torah, the scrolls of which are kept in the ark.

In the synagogue ritual, created by the Rabbis in the generation after the destruction of the Temple, we approach the ark with a song taken from the words of Isaiah (2:3):

> Ki mi-Tzion teitzei Torah, u-devar Adonai
> mi-Yerushalayim.
> *For Torah shall come forth from Zion,*
> *The word of Adonai from Jerusalem.*

The context for this verse is Isaiah's vision of the end of days:

> In the days to come,
>> The Mount of the House of Adonai
>> Shall stand firm above the mountains
>> And tower above the hills;
>> And all the nations
>> Shall gaze on it with joy.
>> And the many peoples shall go and say:
>> "Come,
>> Let us go up to the Mount of Adonai,
>> To the House of the God of Jacob;
>> That God may instruct us in God's ways,
>> And that we may walk in God's paths."
>>> For Torah shall come forth from Zion,
>>> The word of Adonai from Jerusalem.
>> Thus God will judge among the nations
>> And arbitrate for the many peoples,
>> And they shall beat their swords into plowshares
>> And their spears into pruning hooks:
>> Nation shall not take up
>> Sword against nation;
>>> They shall never again know war.
> (Isaiah 2:2–4)

The ritual imagines that as we ascend the steps of the synagogue toward the ark to bring the Torah into the public for reading and study, we are actually rehearsing the day when all humanity shall be brought together to learn divine wisdom. In that day, Torah will belong to all humanity. All humanity will ascend with us to receive Torah. And humanity will bond together to build the world on the model of Eden.

And at the close of the ritual, as the Torah is being returned to its place in the ark, the Rabbis prescribed that we sing of the Torah words taken from the biblical book of Proverbs (3:18):

Eitz chayim hi, le-machazikim bah.
It is a Tree of Life to those who grasp it.

In the Rabbinic imagination, Torah is the Tree of Life. According to Genesis, the Garden of Eden was never destroyed. It may be beyond our reach, guarded by a fearsome angel, but it lives, at least in our dreams. And the Tree of Life still stands in its center. For the Rabbis, Torah is that Tree. It is the core of the dream of Eden, the way back into a world perfected. To learn Torah is to step momentarily back into Eden. To live a life of Torah is to bring Eden to life in the world. To teach Torah is to bring the day Isaiah foretold, the day when the world will be restored to the oneness of Eden.

The day will come, promised the Rabbis, when Torah will become the way of the world, and the world will be restored to the oneness of Eden. Each time the Torah is read in synagogue is one step closer to that dream. That dream enabled the Rabbis to reorganize Jewish life in the wake of its greatest catastrophe.

"MY CHILDREN HAVE DEFEATED ME"

What did God think of all this? Or rather, what idea of God did the Rabbis hold that permitted them this bold creativity? The answer is found in one of the most astonishing legends in the Talmud.[3] The context is a discussion among the Rabbis of the second century—the students of Yochanan ben Zakkai—on the ethics of speech. What kinds of speech are kosher, and what kinds are not? And in the midst of this discussion, a tale is told about an oven, created by an ingenious inventor named Achnai.

In ancient Israel, as in many premodern cultures, a village shared a common oven. Occasionally, a rodent or reptile would crawl into the oven, rendering it unclean. It might take a week or more to cool, clean, and relight the oven. Meanwhile, the village had no bread. Then Achnai the inventor arrived with a solution— the world's first self-cleaning oven: break the tiles of the oven floor and pour sand between the broken pieces; as the oven heats, the sand super-heats, and anything crawling in is incinerated. He brought the design to the Rabbis at Yavneh. Rabbi Eliezer declared his oven pure. The other rabbis rejected the design and declared it impure.

This was highly unusual. Rabbi Eliezer, the brilliant disciple of Yochanan ben Zakkai, was *av beit din*, the second-in-command of the court. Tall and of striking appearance, Rabbi Eliezer retained every truth his teacher ever uttered. No one ever disagreed with him, except this time.

> On that day, Rabbi Eliezer brought forward every imaginable argument, but they [the other rabbis] would not accept them.
>
> Said he to them, "If the *halachah* [law] agrees with me, then let this carob tree prove it!" Thereupon, the carob tree was torn a hundred cubits from its place. Others said it was four hundred cubits. "No proof can be brought from a carob tree," they retorted.
>
> He said to them, "If the *halachah* agrees with me, let the stream of water prove it!" Then, the stream flowed backwards. "No proof can be brought from a stream of water."[4]

Rabbi Eliezer marshaled all his mighty persuasive powers but failed to convince his colleagues. So he produced a miracle. He pointed to the tree in the courtyard, and the tree rocketed high into the air. The Rabbis were indeed impressed. They didn't dispute that this is an awesome miracle. But they refused to yield. "No proof can be brought from a tree!" Failing with the tree, he pointed to the river, and it ran uphill. Again, no dispute that this was a miracle, but "no proof can be brought from a stream."

Why not? After all, there are entire religions based on the sudden and powerful occurrence of miracles. Doesn't this mean that God concurs with him?

The Rabbis realized there was something more at stake than an oven. Who controls our religious life? Who shapes our covenant with God? The Rabbis established a process of legal and moral reasoning for the purpose of interpreting the Torah and applying its ethical and religious rules to the circumstances of life. That process demanded judgment, conscience, and moral imagination. To accept the miracle as authoritative effectively ends the discussion and terminates the process. Reasoning, judgment, and moral intelligence would be silenced. Accept the miracle and Rabbi Eliezer wins, not because his argument was convincing, but by the power and spectacle of his miracle. And therefore he rules. He makes the rules. Authority silences discussion. The freedom of conscience and moral imagination is quashed in the face of the miracle—until someone comes up with a bigger miracle to displace him. The Jewish people began in flight from Pharaoh. Accepting the miracle puts us right back under the thumb of a Pharaoh.

Rabbi Eliezer doesn't understand this. And he loses his temper.

> Again he said to them, "If the *halachah* agrees with me, let the walls of this academy prove it!" Whereupon the walls began to fall over. But Rabbi Joshua rebuked them [the walls], saying, "When scholars are engaged in a halachic dispute, what right have you to interfere?" Hence, they did not fall in honor of Rabbi Joshua, nor did they resume an upright position in deference to Rabbi Eliezer, and thus, to this day, they are still leaning over.[5]

This is a gesture called spite, which is not entirely unknown in Jewish families. Rabbi Eliezer would rather be dead than lose. He would bring down the walls upon the scholars and crush them all to death to prove his point. So Rabbi Joshua intervenes. Rabbi Joshua was the other great disciple of Yochanan ben Zakkai. He was in every sense the opposite of Rabbi Eliezer. While Eliezer was tall and powerful of stature, Joshua was tiny and bent over. Eliezer was wealthy and well-appointed. Joshua was poorer than poor. He earned a livelihood burning charcoal, so he came to the academy covered with soot and grime. But when he taught Torah, he became Eliezer's equal. Rabbi Joshua scolds the walls, but they cannot decide what to do, stand up or fall down? So to this very day, they lean.

In utter frustration, Rabbi Eliezer pulls out his final, ultimate miracle. He brings God as his witness:

> Finally, he said to them, "If the *halachah* agrees with me, let it be proved in heaven!" Whereupon a Heavenly Voice cried out, "Why do you dispute with Rabbi Eliezer? In *all* matters, the *halachah* agrees with him."
>
> Rabbi Joshua arose and exclaimed, "It [Torah] is not in heaven" [Deuteronomy 30:12].[6]

Rabbi Eliezer invokes God, and God comes and validates his position. Game over? Hardly. For up jumps Rabbi Joshua, as it were, to respond with a verse from the very end of the book of Deuteronomy. In that verse, Moses, approaching his death, gives a final charge to his people:

> This commandment that I command you today is not beyond you; it is not far away! It is not in heaven—that you should say, "Who will go up to the heavens and get it for us, and teach it to us, so we can do it?" And it is not across the sea,

that you should say, "Who will cross to the other side and get it for us, and teach it to us, so we can do it?" No! It is very near to you. It is in your mouth and in your heart to do it! (Deuteronomy 30:11–14)

The Torah is not in heaven, nor beyond the sea, nor beyond our reach. The Torah is, in fact, *in us*—in mind and heart and conscience. Torah belongs to us. God has given us the faculties of moral reasoning to interpret and apply it in daily life. And God has given us the authority to do so. In other words, Rabbi Joshua says to God, "Back off! You gave us Torah. You gave us reason and conscience. You told us to teach Torah ... now let us be to do Your will!"

The story ends with a remarkable postscript. According to the Bible, Elijah the prophet never died. He was carried into heaven by a fiery chariot. So in the Jewish imagination, he still lives and visits the world each day to carry out special divine missions. Generations after Rabbi Eliezer and Rabbi Joshua, there lived a mystic, Rabbi Nathan, who had encounters with Elijah.

> Rabbi Nathan met Elijah [the Prophet] and asked him, "What did the Holy One, blessed be God, do at that moment?" "He laughed with joy," he replied, "and said, 'My children have defeated Me, My children have defeated Me.'"[7]

How did God accept all this? Rabbi Nathan wondered. How did God respond to Rabbi Joshua's admonishment? Was God angry? Hurt? Dejected? After all, a God who felt rejected and responded with anger or despair would leave us in a very different religious world. But that is not the God of the Rabbis. Instead, Rabbi Nathan received a remarkable vision: "He laughed with joy, and said, 'My children have defeated Me.'"

The God of the Rabbis celebrates human moral autonomy, human responsibility, human ingenuity. As a parent revels in the growing independence of a child and the flowering of the child's character, the God of the Rabbis revels in our chutzpah. When children surpass us, especially in the skills we taught them, we take pride, not offense. So too, the Rabbis determined, God takes pride in the assertion of our authority to interpret Torah, to do what's right. Therefore, the highest spiritual virtue in Rabbinic Judaism is not obedience, but moral independence.

The story's parental metaphor is poignant. Were we to wait for God's instruction every time we faced a moral dilemma, we would be spiritually infantilized. To seek some powerful authority to answer our questions—an authority whose charisma or magic somehow authenticates their position—is to retreat into spiritual childishness. We mature only when we realize that Torah and its wisdom is not far away, but "in our mouth and in our heart to do it" (Deuteronomy 30:14).

But there is a cost to this. Rabbi Eliezer, it turns out, was right about the oven, and the Rabbis were wrong. Independent moral judgment comes at the cost of ambiguity. In staking our autonomy, we give up certainty. Certainty comes only with the acknowledgment of some authority—when we stop thinking and let some authority think for us. Children have certainty. Adulthood brings us dignity. But adulthood also brings the realization that we're never sure and we might be wrong. Maturity, taught the Rabbis, means trading certainty for the dignity of independence. And God celebrates this in us.

MOSES AND AKIBA: THE CHUTZPAH OF RABBINIC JUDAISM

The chutzpah of the Rabbis is breathtaking. Another classic Rabbinic legend portrays the scene at the top of Mount Sinai when Moses ascends the mountain to receive God's Torah. The Torah scroll is written in a calligraphy that adorns certain letters with

decoration. Legend holds that it was God who invented that calligraphy. When Moses inquires about the meaning of the decorations, he is invited to visit the academy of Rabbi Akiba, who "will
interpret a gigantic mountain of law from each dot." Transported
miraculously to Akiba's academy, Moses is lost in the world of
Akiba's Torah.

> [Moses] found himself sitting in the eighth row of Rabbi
> Akiba's academy. He listened to the rabbi and his disciples but
> could not follow the discussion. He was greatly grieved. But
> just then, he heard one of the disciples question their master
> in regard to a certain point of law: "How do you know this?"
> And he answered, "This is a *halachah* given to Moses on Mount
> Sinai." And now Moses was content. Moses said, "You have a
> man like Akiba, and yet You give the Torah to Israel through
> me?" God answered, "Be silent, so has it been decreed by Me."[8]

Torah was given at Sinai—the Written Torah as well as its interpretation in the Oral Torah. This is the foundational myth of
Rabbinic Judaism. Rabbis, according to this myth, do not create
new religious forms; they merely discover and reveal what was
always present but latent in the Torah text. Rabbis do not legislate;
they only interpret. The source of rabbinic authority is the tradition stretching back to Moses and the Torah he received from God
on Sinai.

All cultures that revere continuity maintain similar beliefs.
Successive generations do not innovate or alter the tradition.
Anything they purport to discover has always been there, waiting to be revealed. This is the myth of continuity. But continuity
is a paradox. Times change. Historical circumstances, technolo-
gies, attitudes, social arrangements, morals, and mores change.
Maintaining continuity in times of change places demands upon
a culture. To maintain continuity, innovation is necessary. That

is, discontinuity is sometimes necessary for the sake of continuity. But how does a culture maintain the authority of continuity in the face of necessary change?

Moses sits in Rabbi Akiba's academy and is baffled by the discussion. Imagine Alexander Hamilton or James Madison coming to visit today's United States Supreme Court. The Supreme Court, after all, is charged with interpreting the Constitution. Would the framers of the Constitution perceive that the issues debated in the Supreme Court today have anything to do with the Constitution they created? Could they follow the discussion? The evolution of a culture, even a culture deeply committed to continuity, strains its foundational myth. Moses is upset. He has no idea what Akiba is talking about. It appears that his people have abandoned his Torah. Then he hears Akiba assert that all this is indeed the Torah "given to Moses on Mount Sinai." Akiba's commitment to the continuity of tradition as the ultimate source of authority comforts Moses. The past is satisfied as long as it still has a voice in the present.

This astonishing legend acknowledges the Rabbis' grasp of this paradox. The legend brings Rabbinic Judaism face to face with its biblical origins: Moses, the greatest prophet of the Bible, the Torah's lawgiver, the paragon of biblical religion, meets Rabbi Akiba, the archetype and quintessence of Rabbinic Judaism.

In Rabbinic literature, Akiba is presented as the total embodiment of Torah. He is the Rabbis' Achilles, the mythic hero who personifies the values and themes of their culture. Akiba, it is told, lived as an illiterate shepherd until he was forty. He surreptitiously married his wealthy employer's beautiful daughter, Rachel, and it was at her strong insistence and through her extraordinary self-sacrifice that he went to learn Torah and became the greatest of the Rabbis. Unlike the Greco-Roman heroes whose gifts are inborn, Torah is available to anyone who has the discipline and desire to learn. And it is never too late to begin. Actually Akiba, having come to Torah only as an adult, possessed the advantage of a child-like wonder for the text.

> Then he went and sat before Rabbi Eliezer and Rabbi Joshua. "My masters, reveal the sense of the Mishnah to me." When they told him one *halachah*, he went off to reason with himself. This *alef*, he wondered, what was it written for? That *bet*, what was it written for? This teaching, what was it uttered for? He kept coming back, kept inquiring of Rabbi Eliezer and Rabbi Joshua, until he reduced his teachers to silence.[9]

For Akiba, nothing in Torah is relegated to mere literary form. Akiba's hermeneutic is rooted in his reverence for the divinity of Torah so that each letter of the Torah is significant and laden with meaning and even the calligraphic decorations carry implication. Here is the paradox of continuity once again: the most passionate champion of Torah, Akiba is Moses's most faithful heir. His devotion to the sanctity of Torah draws him to uncover layers of meaning that even Moses the lawgiver could not have imagined and would not have recognized. Again, the Rabbis recognize the paradox: in the story, Moses is at once baffled, impressed, and humbled. "Be silent!" he is admonished.

The paradox is yet deeper. Akiba's chutzpah in extending the horizons of Torah far beyond Moses's comprehension is an expression of the Bible's vision of the human being as a vessel of divine blessing in the world. Taught Rabbi Akiba:

> Beloved are humans for they were created in the image of God. But it was by a special love that it was made known to them that they were created in the image of God.[10]

According to Talmudic legend, Akiba was once challenged by the Roman governor Turnus Rufus: Which are greater, the works of God or the works of human beings? Akiba's answer surprises the pagan

Rufus. "The works of human beings," he replies. When Rufus protests, Akiba produces a pile of sheaves of wheat and a loaf of bread. Which is greater? inquires Akiba.[11] The blessing prescribed by the Rabbis to begin a meal is *Ha-motzi lechem min ha-aretz,* "Praised is God who brings bread from the earth." We praise God not for wheat but for bread because God is perceived not only in the fertility of nature but also in the human capacity to turn the materials of nature into edible nourishment. According to a later rabbi, "Everything created in the six days of the Creation needs completion: wheat must be milled, mustard and lupine must be sweetened."[12] If wheat must be milled, kneaded, and baked to become bread, so too must Torah be opened, interpreted, and expounded to find its place in the world. In consonance with the biblical ideal, the Rabbis maintain that the creative energies of human beings do not compromise the greatness of God. On the contrary, God celebrates human ingenuity so much that God takes the time to add decorative touches to the letters just so Akiba can find meaning there, generations after Moses.

IMMORTALITY AND ANGUISH

The Greco-Roman hero was tested in war and earned his immortality by dying a spectacular, public death during battle, leaving the poets to recite his tales for generations. Akiba's death is also the summation of his life and the occasion of his immortality in the legends of the Rabbis. In the wake of the failed revolt of Bar Kochba in 135 CE, the Romans outlawed the teaching of Torah. Akiba persisted teaching in public. Torah, he argued, is the source of this people's life.

> If we are fearful when we sit and study the Torah, of which it is written, "For that is your life and the length of your days" (Deuteronomy 30:20), how much more fearful ought we to be should we cease the study of the words of Torah![13]

Akiba was arrested by the Romans. As the spiritual godfather of the Bar Kochba revolt, Akiba was the living symbol of Jewish rebellion. The Romans determined to make an example of him by executing him in public with gruesome torture.

> When Rabbi Akiba was taken out to be executed, it was the hour for the recital of the *Shema*. The executioners were combing his flesh with iron combs, while he was lovingly making himself ready to accept upon himself the yoke of the kingship of heaven [i.e., to recite *Shema Yisrael*, the central Jewish confession of faith].
>
> His disciples asked, "Our teacher, even now [*ad kaan*]?"
>
> He replied, "All my days I have been troubled by this verse, '[Love Adonai your God ...] with all your soul' [Deuteronomy 6:5], which I have interpreted as meaning 'Even if God takes your soul.' But I said, 'When shall I have occasion to fulfill the precept?' Now that I have the occasion, shall I not fulfill it?"
>
> He prolonged the *Shema's* concluding word, *Echad*, "One," until he expired as he finished pronouncing it. A divine voice went forth and proclaimed, "Happy are you, Akiba, that your soul has departed with the word *Echad!*"[14]

In the midst of torture, Akiba discovers an opportunity to demonstrate again that spiritual might can overcome brute force. Akiba turns the act of dying into a moment of teaching. Even death can be redeemed and transformed if it is filled with Torah. Ignoring the physical agony of torture, Akiba revels in the opportunity to reassert his connection to God with the recitation of *Shema Yisrael*. And then, the greatest teacher of Torah turns the moment into a lesson, engaging in a pedagogic dialogue with his students. This is the moment for the revelation of Akiba's greatest truth: no moment is without its Torah. Torah never dies. And one who makes life and even death into a vessel of Torah gains immortality.

Akiba expires with the word *Echad*, "One," on his lips. Despite the brutality that fills the world, the dream of oneness will not die.

Moses, of course, knows nothing of this. Having marveled at Akiba's Torah, he innocently asks to see Akiba's reward.

> Moses then said, "O God of the world, You have permitted me to behold this man's learning; let me see his reward." God said, "Go, return and see." Moses saw the body of the martyred Akiba hanging in the market. He said to God, "Is this the reward for such learning?" God replied, "Be silent; thus have I decreed."[15]

Moses is shown the torn and broken body of Akiba hanging in the marketplace. With indignant poetry he protests, "*Zo Torah, ve-zo secharah?*" Is this the reward for the greatest teacher of Torah? This is the world You created, God? Shall not the Judge of all the earth do justice? Again, he is told to keep silent. Moses complies. And the Rabbis comply. Here the story ends. No protest ensues. There is no resolution, no repair, no *tikkun*. For all their chutzpah, the Rabbis realize they are not Abraham. They are humble in defining the realm of their prerogative. We are back in the world of Job.

In shaping the religious life of the Jewish people, the Rabbis assert breathtaking chutzpah. They appropriate to themselves the prerogative to determine the covenantal relationship with God. And they imagine a God who not only goes along but also celebrates their chutzpah. The power to establish the meaning of Torah belongs to the Rabbis. But the power to determine the political life of the Jewish people—their place in a material world—is left to God. In Torah, the Rabbis are champions. In history, God is the only actor; human beings are but bystanders, waiting for God to bring redemption. And should we rise and protest this fate, God answers, "Be silent; thus have I decreed."

The contrast between Rabbinic chutzpah and Rabbinic passivity infuriates modern Jews. But its effectiveness as a survival strategy cannot be denied. This strategy kept the Jewish people alive for eighteen hundred years of exile, allowing us to absorb catastrophe after catastrophe while remaining culturally creative, flexible, and resilient. In the face of overwhelming Roman power and the staggering losses from military defeat, the Rabbis surrendered the political world to God but maintained a reserve of courage and creativity within the life of the spirit.

Nevertheless, they preserved the words of Moses's anguish:

Zo Torah, ve-zo secharah?
This is the life of Torah, and this is its fate in the world?

Moses's protest is not answered. But neither is it erased. God demands silence. But silence doesn't become Jews. They will not take back power in the world of politics for some eighteen hundred years. But they will find other ways to answer. For this people's character is chutzpah.

Chapter Five

RETURNING TO THE GARDEN

> This is the word of Adonai to Zerubbabel: Not by might, not by
> power, but by My spirit—said Adonai of Hosts. (Zechariah 4:6)

The postexilic prophet Zechariah faced a despondent people with a defeated leader, the governor, Zerubbabel. The community had returned to Jerusalem with the permission of the Persian king but was soon overwhelmed by the tasks of rebuilding the city and its Temple and restoring the glory of the broken Jerusalem. They fought stiff opposition from the local population. And they fought back the sad recognition that nothing they built could live up to the Jerusalem of their dreams. The prophet's words (made famous by the popular Debbie Freidman song) sought to reframe the task. The Temple's glory came neither from the physical structure nor from the power of the state that built it, but from the presence of the Divine that dwelled within. And the prophet proclaimed his confidence that if they built it, God would come.

Ironically, this is the prophetic selection, the haftarah, chosen by the Rabbis of the Talmud to be read on the Sabbath of Hanukkah. Hanukkah celebrates the greatest military victory achieved by the

Jewish people since Joshua conquered Canaan, and the only victory until the 1948 Israeli War of Independence. But the Rabbis chose this message. This people's power is not in military might, nor in political control, but in the life of the spirit. With these words, the Rabbis announce the Jewish exit from history, slamming the door behind them.

This was not, however, the end of chutzpah. For the Rabbis, Hanukkah celebrates the miracle of light—the persistent power of Torah's light to illuminate a dark and cruel world. Yochanan ben Zakkai fled the defense of Jerusalem to establish the academy of Yavneh. Akiba taught Torah under the threat of death, and even in death, he continued to teach his Torah. The trek from Egypt to Eden was not abandoned. It was relocated from history to spirit, from the life of nations to the life of the mind and heart. Torah became the territory of Jewish life. The heroic spirit of chutzpah was sublimated into the life of learning.

"THE TEXT CRIES OUT, 'INTERPRET ME!'"

"Chumash with Rashi" has been the core of traditional Jewish literacy since the eleventh century. "Chumash with Rashi" is the Torah with the commentary of Rabbi Shlomo ben Yitzchak, abbreviated as "Rashi," who lived in Troyes, in the north of France, 1040–1104. Rashi chose carefully from the vast ocean of Rabbinic teaching to convey the core traditions a Jew needs to know. His choices of citations divulge the character of his own religious life. So authoritative was this commentary that it was the first Hebrew work ever printed, and since then, it has typically been printed adjacent to the Torah text itself, so that they form a dialogue on the page. Rashi's terse style, his spare language, has inspired more than two hundred "super-commentaries" expounding his intentions and insights.

In his very first commentary, on the Bible's opening verse, Rashi reveals the essence of medieval Jewish spirituality.

In the beginning, God created the heaven and the earth.
(Genesis 1:1)

> Rabbi Isaac taught: The Torah should have begun with
> the verse "This month shall mark for you the beginning of the
> months ..." (Exodus 12:2), which is the first commandment
> given to Israel. For what reason does the Torah begin with
> Genesis [or: Creation]?

Rashi opens his commentary with a popular midrash from the
collection *Tanchuma*, which poses a question so obvious it is
never asked: Why begin with Genesis? Upon reflection, the question turns out to be quite remarkable, and that itself is a lesson.
Questions matter. The beginning of wisdom is asking the right
question. The world of traditional Jewish learning rewards students for important questions even more than clever answers.
When we went into exile from our homeland, truth went into exile
as well. Posing the right question is a step toward redemption.

Why begin with Genesis? Most great books don't begin at the
beginning. They begin somewhere in the middle of a story and
flash backward.

"Call me Ishmael."

"It was the best of times, it was the worst of times."

"If you really want to hear about it, the first thing you'll prob-
ably want to know is where I was born, and what my lousy
childhood was like...."

The Bible is one of the very few that actually opens with the beginning. But the beginning of what?

Rabbi Isaac wonders why the Torah didn't open with Exodus
12, the first commandment given to Israel, the commandment to
keep a Jewish calendar. Why does the Torah begin with universal
time instead of Jewish time?

Had the Torah begun with Exodus 12, what would we lose? The Creation; Adam and Eve, Cain and Abel; Noah; the patriarchs and matriarchs; Joseph and his brothers; the slavery of Egypt, the early life of Moses, the beginning of the liberation. We would lose all the Bible's best stories. Exodus 12 is our first law. Were the Bible a collection of legislation, it would have begun with Exodus 12. The presence of all that comes before Exodus 12 testifies that the Bible is much more than law. There is law in the Bible, but law must be rooted in narrative. Narrative establishes the world in which law lives. Narrative gives the law meaning and purpose. Judaism is not just law, but a vision of the world and our place in it. To build Jewish life solely on law is to tear Genesis out of the Torah.

Exodus 12 isn't even the Torah's first commandment. The Torah's first commandment is "Be fruitful and multiply" (Genesis 1:28). This commandment was given to Adam and Eve, progenitors of all humanity. Exodus 12, as Rabbi Isaac notes, is the first commandment given *to Israel*. So, whose Bible is this? Is this a truth shared with all humanity, or is this the provenance of the Jewish people alone? Is the Torah a truth that speaks to the human condition we share with all, or does it speak solely to the particular experience of being Jewish? If Torah spoke only to the Jew in us and had nothing to say to the human being in us, it would have begun with Exodus 12. The presence of Genesis is a proclamation of the Bible's universality.

The Bible has no "reader's introduction," no preface, not even a title page. The Bible provides no instruction on what it is and how it is to be read. It is a completely unself-conscious text. Rashi's first comment corrects this. With deft subtlety, he pushes aside generations of dispute, setting an environment of learning that welcomes narrative as well as law, speaks to the universal as well as the particular, and warmly celebrates questioning. This is Rashi's chutzpah.

Rashi then brings Rabbi Isaac's answer:

Because of [the thought expressed in Psalm 111:6] "God
revealed to God's people God's powerful works in giving
them the heritage of the nations." For should the people of
the world say to them, "You are robbers because you took by
force the land of the seven nations [of Canaan]," Israel may
reply to them, "All the earth belongs to the Holy One, blessed
be God; God created it and gave it to whom God shall choose.
It was according to God's will that God gave it to them, and
now, it is according to God's will that God takes it from them
and gives it to us."

The answer is decidedly less ingenious than the question. Genesis,
it seems, is in the Bible to justify the Israelite conquest of Canaan.
It's a political text. But Rashi, living in France and witnessing
the massacres of the First Crusade, has to realize the weakness of
the argument. Both the crusaders and their Moslem opponents
believed God gave the Holy Land to them. Everyone believes God
is on their side. Rashi's real intentions can only be discerned when
we look at the context of the proof text in Psalm 111:4–10.

> *Adonai is gracious and compassionate;*
> *God gives food to those who fear God;*
> *God is ever mindful of God's covenant.*
> *God revealed to God's people God's powerful works,*
> *in giving them the heritage of nations.*
> *God's handiwork is truth and justice; all God's precepts are*
> *enduring,*
> *well-founded for all eternity, wrought of truth and equity.*
> *God sent redemption to God's people; God ordained God's*
> *covenant for all time;*
> *God's name is holy and awesome.*

The beginning of wisdom is the fear of Adonai;
all who practice it gain sound understanding.
Praise of God is everlasting.

Rabbi Isaac took the phrase "the heritage of nations" to mean the land of Canaan. But the psalm identifies God's works with truth, precepts, and wisdom. This is Rashi's message: Let Christians and Moslems tear themselves apart in battle for the Holy Land. It is the deluded fantasy of powerful men to imagine they control the destiny of that land. God controls that land. God will take it and give it as God wills. This we Jews have learned the hard way. Our legacy is no longer that land, but something far more valuable— divine truth. Our spiritual home is Torah. And that can never be taken from us.

With this introduction, Rashi turns to the text itself. The book of Genesis begins with an egregious grammatical error. The very first word, *Bereishit*, is in the construct form, "In the beginning of." Grammatically, the next word must be a noun, as in "In the beginning of time" or "In the beginning of the world." But in the text of the Torah as it is traditionally read, the next word is a verb, *bara*, literally, "He created." Rashi comments, "*Bereishit bara*, this verse calls out, '*Darsheini*! Interpret me!'"

In a comment that appears later in Genesis, Rashi states his intention to bring the *peshat*—the simple meaning—of the Torah text. But the simple meaning is not a literal reading.

The world is full of believers who claim the literal meaning of the Bible. This literal meaning, they maintain, is objective and authoritative—it is what the text says; any other reading is embellishment or corruption. To read scripture, they believe, is to passively receive God's truth. God speaks, we listen. God instructs, we learn. God commands, we obey. God is pure, humanity is compromised; the domain of divine wisdom must be shielded from unclean human hands. The commitment to a literal reading provides them a sense of security that their religion is genuine, timeless, and true beyond any mere human truth. Read literally, the text offers absolute truth.

In this brief, sly comment, Rashi responds: There is no such thing as a literal reading of the Bible! The very first words of the Bible, read literally, are indecipherable. From its very first word, the Bible text cannot be read without interpretation. Without interpretation, the words of the Bible have no meaning. Moreover, the Bible was never intended to be read this way. The words themselves cry out, "Interpret me!" Reading is not a passive process. Truth is never passively received. Meaning is revealed only when the reader engages the texts as an active partner in constructing its meaning.

Rashi's observation derives from his very Jewish estimation of the human being, from his chutzpah. "The human being," observed the ancient Rabbis, "is God's partner in the project of Creation."[1] The human being is God's partner in the creation of Torah's meaning. Revelation, the delivery of God's word to the world, is not a process of passive reception, but of active construction. The watchword of Jewish faith, "Shema Yisrael—Listen, Israel!" (Deuteronomy 6:4), demands not docile obedience, but a transaction, a dynamic engagement between the reader and the word.

The construction of meaning through interpretation involves judgment. And judgment introduces subjectivity into the text. Different readers will disagree about the correct interpretation. The process of reading with interpretation always entails debate. Torah is not the book inertly lying on the table. Torah is the passionate debate that goes on above the book. God may once have spoken the words of Torah. But when they enter our world, they split and refract into the tensions and dialectic that are the heart of passionate Torah learning. There is no absolute certainty in the realm of Torah; no one can claim the final interpretation. Instead of certainty, there is the dignity of sharing the task of discovering truth. Every active reader is entitled to that dignity.

Rashi was one of the first to author a running commentary on Torah. His is certainly the paradigm for all later commentaries. The literary form of commentary bespeaks a way of appropriating tradition, which is best visualized on a page of a traditional Bible. The Torah text is printed at the center. The Torah text is authoritative. But it cannot be read alone. Commentary surrounds and embraces the text. Then there are commentaries on commentaries. Commentary opens the meaning of the text. Revelation, God's word, resides in the conversation, the debate, between yesterday and today. The commentary is at once traditional and original— innovative, creative, even revolutionary, while keeping faith with the received legacy.

Rashi concludes his comment with two suggested readings:

> If we wish to understand the simple meaning of the text, we would read as follows: "At the beginning of God's creation of heaven and earth [in Hebrew: *Bereishit bero Elohim*], the earth was unformed and void."
>
> If we wish to follow the Rabbis in their interpretive understanding of the text, we would read: "For the sake of the Torah, God created the heavens and the earth." [*Reishit* refers to the Torah,] as in the verse in Proverbs 8:22, "Adonai created me [i.e., Torah] as the beginning [*reishit*] of God's way."

To read the text literally, Rashi suggests we alter its grammar, changing the second word from a verb (*bara*) to a noun (*bero*). This makes the entire first verse into a subjunctive clause, "At the beginning of God's creation of heaven and earth, the earth was unformed and void." Actually rewriting the biblical text, Rashi demonstrates, is the only way to read the Torah text literally.

Ironically, pursuing a literal reading demands the more radical act of textual reconstruction to bring meaning to the text.

By contrast, Rashi suggests the interpretive reading of the Talmudic Rabbis: *bereishit* means "for the Torah." The Torah's first line proclaims: For the sake of Torah was the world created. What you hold in your hands is nothing less than the blueprint of the created universe. This is an apt first line of the book. Torah, it affirms, is the primary reality. The world is only its setting. To engage Torah is to engage the very source and essence of all reality. Torah is life. To engage Torah is the purpose of existence. It is the highest expression of one's humanity. In this brief comment, Rashi welcomes us to the world of medieval Judaism. The human being, as student of Torah, has the capacity to commune with God, to read the thoughts and intentions of the Creator through the sacred scripture. No other pursuit could be more important. And Rashi offers his services as our guide.

THE PERFECTION OF THE MIND IS THE PRESENCE OF GOD

The student came to the master on a spiritual quest. The master tutored him in natural sciences, logic, and mathematics. The student bristled. When will we talk of God, of faith, of revelation? The master questioned and challenged him relentlessly—turning, and overturning all the accepted tenets of his received tradition. The student rebelled. When will you reveal your truth? At long last, the master offered a parable.

> I shall begin the discourse in this chapter with a parable that
> I shall compose for you: The ruler is in his palace, and all his
> subjects are partly within the city and partly outside the city.
> Of those who are within the city, some have turned their backs
> upon the ruler's habitation, their faces being turned another

way. Others seek to reach the ruler's habitation, turn toward it, and desire to enter it and to stand before him, but up to now they have not yet seen the wall of the habitation. Some of those who seek to reach it have come up to the habitation and walk around it searching for its gate. Some of them have entered the gate and walk about in the antechambers. Some of them have entered the inner court of the habitation and have come to be with the king, in one and the same place with him, in the ruler's habitation. But their having come into the inner part of the habitation does not mean that they see the ruler or speak to him. For after their coming into the inner part of the habitation, it is indispensable that they should make another effort; then they will be in the presence of the ruler, see him from afar or from nearby, or hear the ruler's speech or speak to him.[2]

If it is God you truly seek, know this: The Ruler resides in the palace in the heart of the city. God is not far away. God lives right here, at the center of our reality. The Ruler invites us to an audience. God beckons. It is the epitome of human existence, its highest purpose and greatest joy, to stand in the presence of God, to know God. The pathway to God's presence is the cultivation of mind, the discovery of truth. There is no shortcut. To know God is to understand all of reality. To know God, you must master all there is to know. Of all God's creatures the human being alone was given the divine gift of reason, and through reason, we can discover truth. We possess the capacity to know God. Knowing God lies within the potential of human beings. But very few will ever realize their potential. Whether you succeed in your search for God is entirely a question of your own preparation, your persistence, your powers of mind and will and desire.

Look out at the world, the master instructed. Most of humanity lives outside the city, oblivious to the Ruler within. They pursue purposes unrelated to the Ruler's presence. They are human only in outer form. Pursuing the pleasures of the body and satisfied with the mindless, unreflective life, they are more animal than human.

Believers possessed of wrong opinions are those who live in the city but are turned away from the Ruler. With each act of devotion, they distance themselves from the Ruler's palace. Bad religion, like bad medicine, is practiced with good intentions but without wisdom and without skill. It brings no health and no wholeness.

Those who face the right direction but cannot perceive the palace represent the masses who practice correct religion but never ask why. Out of loyalty to tradition, obedience to authority, or fear of punishment and anticipation of reward, they observe rites and rituals correctly but with no understanding of religion's purposes or principles. Authority has wrung the curiosity out of their religious lives. They value obedience instead of truth. Their tradition functions as a true moral code, but not as a source of enlightenment. It governs the workings of society, providing justice, order, and stability, but leads no one closer to the presence of God.

Similarly, there are some who approach the palace but cannot find the front door. These are the teachers of tradition—the religious specialists—expert in law and practice, but oblivious to the higher purposes and principles of religious life. Consumed with the details of religious legislation—the particulars of the permitted and the forbidden—they are blind to the true purposes of religious life. Law is valued for its own sake without regard for its role in the development of character and consciousness.

All of these account for the masses of humanity and the majority of the Jewish people. That leaves only a very few who question and search and yearn for truth. Only they enter the palace and begin the quest to enter into the chambers of the Ruler. Judaism is not identity, or ethnicity, or nationality, or culture, or even religion. Judaism is a pathway to truth, a way to the perfection of the human being. It is an invitation to stand in presence of God, a guide to the Ruler's inner chamber.

The parable overturned all of Jewish intellectual life. The book was banned and burned all over Europe. But it could not be ignored, because its author was the greatest rabbi and Jewish thinker who ever lived, Moses ben Maimon, Maimonides, known in tradition as the Rambam. Maimonides's towering figure illuminates the entire landscape of medieval Judaism and all of Judaism since. To this day, no element of Jewish life escapes his influence. Tradition exalts, "From Moses to Moses, there is none like Moses."

Maimonides was born in Cordoba in 1138, at the end of the golden age of Spanish Jewish civilization. With the rise of the militant Berber Almohads in 1148, Jewish life in Spain became precarious. Maimonides's family left Cordoba, wandering for some years before settling in Fez, Morocco, and then in Fostat, near Cairo in Egypt. When his brother David, a merchant, was lost at sea during an expedition to India, the family lost their accumulated wealth, and Maimonides his means of support. He took up the position of physician to the court of the grand vizier and the sultan, at the same time serving the Jewish community as its *nagid*, political head, rabbi, as well as resident physician. With all this, Maimonides authored numerous treatises on natural sciences and philosophy, *teshuvot*—appellate decisions in Jewish law—and letters to students the world over. He died in 1204. Tradition maintains that he is buried in Tiberias in Israel.

In Jewish tradition, Maimonides is renown for two works: *Mishneh Torah*, the code of Jewish law and practice he authored in his youth, and *Guide for the Perplexed*, the philosophical masterwork he authored at the end of his life.

In his introduction to *Mishneh Torah*, Maimonides explains his intention:

In our time, severe troubles come one after another, and all
are in distress; the wisdom of our sages has disappeared, and
the understanding of our discerning men is hidden. Thus, the
commentaries, the responses to questions, and the settled laws
that the [Rabbis] wrote, which had once seemed clear, have
in our times become hard to understand, so that only a few
properly understand them.... For this reason, I, Moshe son of
Rabbi Maimon the Sephardi, found that the current situation
is unbearable; and so, relying on the help of the Rock blessed
be He, I intently studied all these books, for I saw fit to write
what can be determined from all of these works in regard to
what is forbidden and permitted, and unclean and clean, and
the other rules of the Torah: Everything in clear language and
terse style, so that the whole Oral Law would become thor-
oughly known to all.[3]

Maimonides was the first scholar to attempt such a massive feat—
to distill all the diverse and contentious traditions of Jewish law
and practice into a clear, well-ordered, concise code. The work
he created was so compelling he claimed that from now on a Jew
need own only two books: the Torah of Moses, and the *Mishneh
Torah*—or Second Torah—of Moses Maimonides. That's chutzpah! And for the most part, he succeeded. *Mishneh Torah* is the
model for every subsequent codification of Jewish law, and it is the
core of the traditional Rabbinic learning.

Maimonides opens his *Mishneh Torah* with a section titled
Sefer Mada, "Book of Knowledge," which in turn opens with
an enumeration of *Hilchot Yesodei Ha-Torah*, "Laws on the
Foundations of Torah." Maimonides maintains that right behavior begins with right beliefs. Law must be rooted in narrative and
worldview, which are as normative as the practices and behaviors
dictated by law. Narrative establishes the authority of the law. But

its role is even more important. Maimonides understands that law serves a purpose loftier than merely regulating human behavior. Law is pedagogic. Law forms character. Law forms the individual and shapes society. Law points toward an ideal personality. Therefore, our beliefs, personal values, and attitudes fall legitimately within the purview of law.

The paradigm shift of *Mishneh Torah* is signaled from its very first words:

> The basic principle of all principles and the foundation of all wisdom is to know that there is a Primary Being who brought into being all existence. All the beings of the heavens, the earth, and what is between them came into existence only from the truth of God's being.[4]

Rashi began his commentary wondering why Torah begins with Genesis. Maimonides begins prior to that. What must one need to know even to open the Torah? Undergirding the entirety of Torah, there is a single, inescapable premise—the existence of God. To define that premise, however, Maimonides resorts to philosophical language. He sounds much more like Aristotle than any text of biblical or Rabbinic teaching. Here begins the new paradigm. Philosophy may have come from outside the Jewish world, but philosophy is now indispensable to the life of Torah. Philosophy is the most effective tool for setting the foundations of Torah with certainty.

In *Mishneh Torah*'s opening words, authored in the early years of his career, Maimonides signals the intellectual dilemma that will follow him his entire life. The existence of the "Primary Being" (*matzui rishon*) is "basic principle of principles" (*yesod ha-yesodot*) and "the foundation of all wisdom" (*amud ha-hoch-mot*). The duplication of language is not just hyperbole. Nothing in Maimonides is simple rhetoric. The "principle of principles" indicates a postulate of reason. Without this idea, nothing else makes sense. The "foundation of all wisdom" means a tenet of tradition, the basis of faith. The reality of the Primary Being is arrived at in two ways, through reason and through tradition. It is the meeting place of these two ways of knowing. How far can Maimonides go in harmonizing these two voices within him—the voice of reason and the voice of tradition? What happens when they conflict? It is this dilemma that will drive him to create the greatest work of Jewish philosophy ever written, the magisterial *Guide for the Perplexed*.

Guide for the Perplexed is a letter from Maimonides to his student, Joseph. Joseph was the prized student Maimonides had waited a lifetime to teach. When Joseph was forced to depart the master in the middle of his training, Maimonides composed the *Guide* to complete their unfinished conversation. A gifted student of philosophy, Joseph could not reconcile his philosophical learning with the Judaism he practiced. The dilemma pulled him apart. He could deny his Judaism out of philosophical skepticism. Or he could discard his philosophical acumen out of loyalty to his faith. Or he could compartmentalize and isolate the two from one another. Anguished by the conflict within him, Joseph came to Maimonides, the physician of the soul.

The good doctor Maimonides threw away these simplistic formulae. Judaism is valuable because it is true. And that truth can be proven by philosophy. There is only one truth. Reason and revelation, science and scripture, must reach the same truth. The project of the *Guide* is to demonstrate this.

Maimonides begins where Rashi began, with the language of the Bible. The language of the Bible is mythical. It does not bear philosophical scrutiny. In the first part of the *Guide*, Maimonides offers a glossary of biblical terms, which effectively reshapes the way we read biblical text. His opening sets the task with exquisite clarity.

"Image" (*tzelem*) and "likeness" (*demut*). People have thought that in the Hebrew language "image" denotes the shape and configuration of a thing. This supposition led them to the doctrine of the corporeality of God, on account of God's saying: "Let us make man in our image, after our likeness" (Genesis 1:26). For they thought that God has a man's form, his shape and configuration. The doctrine of the corporeality of God was a necessary conclusion. They accordingly believed in it and deemed that if they abandoned this belief, they would give the lie to the biblical text....

The term "image" is applied to the nature of a thing—the way a thing constituted as a substance becomes what it is. It is the true reality of the thing. In man, it is that from which intellect derives. It is on account of this intellectual ability that it is said of man: "In the image of God did God create him" (Genesis 1:27).

That which was meant in the scriptural dictum "Let us make man in our image" (Genesis 1:26) was the specific form, which is intellectual capability, not the shape and configuration.... Now man possesses something in him that is unique, as it is not found in anything else that exists under heaven, namely, intellectual capacity.... It was because of the divine intellect conjoined with man that it is said of the latter that he is "in the image of God and in God's likeness" (Genesis 1:26).[5]

The Torah teaches that human beings are created in God's image. So faithful readers of scripture took this as literally true and concluded: If we have bodies, God must have a body. God's body must look like ours, only much bigger. After all, they pointed out, the Bible frequently refers to "the hand of God," "the face of God," and other physical attributes. To deny the corporeality of God is to deny the clear meaning of the Torah text.

The argument over the corporeality of God is Maimonides's doorway into a new Judaism. The corporeality of God, he argues, is a logical impossibility. Any body, any physical object in space, has boundaries. Any body has its limitations, what it can and cannot do. To ascribe corporeality to God is to believe that God is located in one place but not in another, that God is capable of certain things but not others. It is to deny God's infinite being, God's infinite power, and God's perfection. It is to deny that God is God.

There is a moral problem as well. The desire to imagine God as corporeal reflects a deep human need to project ourselves onto God—to make God over in our image. We imagine that God holds our loyalties, our prejudices, our biases. Then we reappropriate these same qualities and deem them sacred. We must be right— God is on our side! Projecting ourselves onto God is idolatry. Abolishing idolatry was Maimonides great passion. A true belief in God draws us out of our narrowness to grasp the world with an ever-expanding vision.

All references in the Bible to God's physicality or other human qualities should be read as metaphor. But metaphor is dangerous. As Rashi realized, introducing interpretation, especially metaphor, into the study of Bible induces a sense of insecurity among a certain class of believers. Losing the literal meaning of the text denies them the confidence that they hold a received, revealed, transcendent truth. How can this be God's word when mere human beings construct and construe its meaning? Rashi demonstrated that is the only way to locate meaning in the text. The Torah was given to us to interpret. It calls out, "*Darsheini!*—Interpret me!" Maimonides goes further. To insist on a belief that is logically impossible because it is written in the Bible is insulting. Nothing in scripture can contradict what we know to be true by logic or science. We don't tolerate, much less venerate, irrationality in other domains of human life; why would we abide it in religion? We are intelligent people. Our religion should be intelligent as well.

How shall the text be read? The image of a thing, Maimonides teaches, is not its appearance but its essence, what makes it what it is uniquely. The unique essence of the human being is reason. This is what we share with God. When we reason with pure, unprejudiced, focused thought, we commune with the mind of God. Reason is a form of revelation. This is the unique gift of God to the human species. Reason is the bridge between the human being and God. This conviction introduces the entire argument of the *Guide.*

At the conclusion of his parable, Maimonides reveals to his student the pathway of religious illumination, the way to the presence of God.

> Those who have plunged into speculation concerning the fundamental principles of religion have entered the antechambers. People there indubitably have different ranks. He, however, who has achieved demonstration, to the extent that that is possible, of everything that may be demonstrated; and who has ascertained in divine matters, to the extent that that is possible, everything that may be ascertained; and who has come close to certainty in those matters in which one can only come close to it—has come to be with the ruler in the inner part of the habitation....
>
> There are those who set their thought to work after having attained perfection in the divine science, turn wholly toward God, may God be cherished and held sublime, renounce what is other than God, and direct all the acts of their intellect toward an examination of the beings with a view to drawing from them proof with regard to God, so as to know God's governance of them in whatever way it is possible. These people

are those who are present in the ruler's council. This is the rank
of the prophets.[6]

Cultivating the life of the mind is the way to God. Intellectual
integrity—holding only those beliefs that have been carefully
examined and proved—is the key to God's inner chamber. A thor-
ough knowledge of the world, which reveals the divine wisdom
governing all things, is the doorway into the ruler's council. This
is the essence of prophecy. Prophecy is not a supernatural endow-
ment. Prophecy is an achievement. Prophecy is attained by those
fervently devoted to the pursuit of truth through the cultivation
of mind.

In Maimonides's vision, the Garden of Eden exists. Eden, the
state of oneness with God, resides in the perfection of the human
mind. There is no fearsome angel holding us out. Entrance to
the Garden is only a matter of human will—mustering the devotion to cultivate the mind. In Maimonides's Garden, the Tree of
Knowledge and Eternal Life is no longer forbidden. On the contrary, sharing the sacred fruit of knowledge and eternity is all God
wants of us. It is the fulfillment of human existence.

The human being is a self-creating, self-perfecting creature,
the only one in all God's creation. Cultivating the life of the mind
is the true essence of being human. This requires certain conditions. The true function of Torah law is to create these conditions.
Intellectual life demands freedom from hunger, thirst, discom-
fort, and dislocation, a freedom available only in a stable, ordered
society. Creating such a society is the first function of Torah law.
The life of the mind demands freedom from the distractions of the
body. This is the product of moral discipline, the next function of
Torah law. Finally, the pursuit of intellectual perfection demands
freedom from mental distraction, the freedom of the disciplined
mind. This, too, is the function of Torah. Every law of the Torah

tradition can be traced back to these functions. Each is necessary, and each is rational. Maimonides demanded intelligent religion. He had no patience for those who found divinity only in the mysterious and the irrational.

> There are people who find it difficult to give a reason for any of the commandments and consider it right to assume that the commandments and prohibitions have no rational basis whatever. They are led to adopt this theory by a certain disease in their soul.... They imagine that if these commandments were useful in any respect and were commanded because of their usefulness, they would seem to originate in the thought and reason of some intelligent being. But [only] things that are not reasonable and serve no purpose undoubtedly come from God, because no thought of man could have produced them.... Surely God is greater than this! On the contrary, the sole object of the law is to benefit us.... Every one of the 613 commandments serves to inculcate some truth, to remove some erroneous opinion, to establish proper relations in society, to diminish evil, to train in good manners, or to warn against bad habits. All this depends on three things: opinions, moral qualities, and civil conduct.... These three principles suffice for assigning a reason for every one of the divine commandments.[7]

Given the gifts of freedom and with suitable natural constitution, a human being with sufficient motivation has the capacity to achieve intellectual perfection and come to understand the universe. This was the singular achievement of Moses, the most realized human being who ever lived. Disciplined of mind and body and naturally gifted, Moses attained the epitome of human existence, standing with God face-to-face. This is why Torah, the law of Moses, is the most perfect law.

Moses fascinates Maimonides. As his namesake, he modeled his life after Moses—lawgiver, teacher, leader, healer. Moses's ascent of the mountain to stand with God is Maimonides's metaphor for the philosophical quest for perfection of the mind, the ideal of a human life. But one important fact of Moses's story vexed Maimonides's carefully drawn vision—Moses comes down the mountain. Standing face-to-face with God, achieving all that a human being yearns for, Moses attains the full perfection of a human being. Then Moses descends to his people, and all their trouble. Why doesn't Moses stay on the mountaintop with God?

Guide for the Perplexed is a massive work. For the entirety of the *Guide,* Maimonides leads his student up the mountain, insisting that standing at the top, in the presence of God, is the goal of human life. The famous parable ends when the seeker finds himself "in the presence of the Ruler." But on the very last page, he produces a surprise.

On the last page, Maimonides returns to the most basic question: What is human life for?

The thinkers of antiquity and modernity, he offers, taught that there are four kinds of perfection that human beings pursue as the purpose of their lives.[8]

The first is the acquisition of wealth, power, and prestige. Although this is the most popular conception of the purpose of life and the goal toward which most human beings aspire, this notion of perfection is false. Wealth, power, and prestige are transient and remain external to the selfhood of a person. What we own is not what we are. And at any moment, a twist of fate can take it all away: "[Even a] great king may one morning find that there is no difference between him and the lowest person."[9]

The second kind of perfection is the perfection of the body. Physical health and beauty come second among the most popular measures of human value. Physical well-being comes closer to self than the acquisition of wealth, and inasmuch as it includes the moderation of bodily desires, it is useful in the pursuit of higher perfections. But as a human purpose, it is empty, because it affects only the body, that which we share with all animals, and not the soul, the essence of the human being.

The third perfection is moral perfection, the cultivation of character. This is the principle aim of the Torah's commandments. By regulating the relations among people, the commandments produce social harmony. As such, they have real utility, but only in the service of higher purposes. Imagine, Maimonides offers, a person stranded alone, apart from any human contact. In that circumstance, a perfected moral character has little use. Morality is necessary and useful, but it is not the highest purpose of human life.

Finally, Maimonides arrives at the conclusion:

> The fourth kind of perfection is the true perfection of man; the possession of the highest intellectual faculties; the possession of such knowledge that leads to true knowledge of God. With this perfection man has obtained his final object. This is true human perfection; it remains to him alone; it gives him immortality, and on its account he is called man.... Your aim must therefore be to attain this [fourth] perfection.[10]

As he has taught so many times in the *Guide,* the cultivation of mind is the true purpose of human existence. On this, the prophets and the philosophers agree. Reason and revelation reach the same vision of human perfection. As a proof text, Maimonides cites the prophet Jeremiah:

> Thus said Adonai:
>> Let not the wise man glory in his wisdom;
>> Let not the strong man glory in his strength;
>> Let not the rich man glory in his riches.

But only in this should one glory:

In his earnest devotion to Me.

For I Adonai act with kindness, justice, and righteous-

ness in the world;

For in these I delight.

(Jeremiah 9:22–23)

The prophet, Maimonides notes, arranges the perfections in the ascending order of their importance in the eyes of most people—first riches, then strength, then wisdom. The prophet affirms that only devotion to God is worthy of glory. But that is not all the prophet says. And here is Maimonides's surprise.

> The prophet does not content himself with explaining that the knowledge of God is the highest kind of perfection; for if this only had been his intention, he would have said, "But only in this should one glory: In his earnest devotion to Me," and would have stopped there.... He says, however, that man can only glory in the knowledge of God and in the knowledge of God's ways and attributes, which are God's actions....
>
> We are thus told in this passage that the divine acts that ought to be known and ought to serve as a guide for our actions are *chesed*, kindness, *mishpat*, justice, and *tzedakah*, righteousness....
>
> The object of the passage is therefore to declare that the perfection in which man can truly glory is attained by him when he has acquired—as far as this is possible for man—the knowledge of God, the knowledge of God's providence, and of the manner in which God brings creatures into being and governs them. Having acquired this knowledge, [the perfected human being] will then be determined always to seek kindness, justice, and righteousness and to imitate the ways of God.[11]

On the last page, the last paragraphs of the *Guide*, Maimonides reveals that the ultimate purpose of human existence is not the perfection of mind and communion with God. Had this been so, Moses would have stayed on the mountaintop. Achieving this pinnacle, the perfected human being will be determined not just to know God, but to imitate the ways of God in the world. Knowledge of God brings responsibility, the obligation to care for the world. The true object of human development is to share the divine qualities of *chesed, mishpat,* and *tzedakah* with the world. It is not sufficient to find the way into Eden just to taste the sacred fruit of knowledge and eternity. Having accomplished this, we acquire the obligation to bring Eden into the world—to be a blessing. This constitutes true human perfection. This celebration of human responsibility is Maimonides' chutzpah.

ENTERING THE INNER LIFE OF GOD

Rabbi Oshaya opened: "Then I was with God, as *amon*; and I was daily all delight" (Proverbs 8:30). [What does the word *amon* mean?] *Amon* is an artisan (*uman*).

The Torah declares, "I was the working tool of the Holy One, blessed be God." In human practice, when a king builds a palace, he builds it not with his own skill but with the skill of an architect. The architect moreover does not build it out of his head, but employs plans and diagrams to know how to arrange the chambers and the doors.

Thus God consulted the Torah and created the world, so that the Torah declares, "*Bereishit* God created ..." (Genesis 1:1). *Reishit* refers to the Torah, as in the verse, "Adonai made me as the beginning [*reishit*] of God's way" (Proverbs 8:22).[12]

In the Talmudic-era sermon, the rabbi played a game with his audience. He threw out an obscure verse far from the text of the weekly lesson. Then, to the delight of the congregation, he skillfully wove his way back in as few steps as possible. This displayed the virtuosity of the rabbi as an expositor of the text, at the same time demonstrating the unity of the biblical text. In this, the very first midrash in the classic fifth-century collection *Bereishit Rabbah,* Rabbi Oshaya begins his interpretation of the opening of Genesis with a verse in the book of Proverbs, "I was with God, as *amon.*" In Proverbs, the speaker of this line is Wisdom, which the Talmudic Rabbis took for Torah. The question is, what does the word *amon* mean? After reviewing a dozen alternatives, Rabbi Oshaya offers this meaning: *amon* is a builder, or better, the builder's plans. Thus the Torah declares, "Before there was anything, I was with God." Torah is the blueprint of the universe. So the first verse of the Torah can be read, "*Bereishit*—With the Torah, God created heaven and earth."

In only two steps, Rabbi Oshaya connects the verses. But more, he opens a door to a revolutionary world of Jewish wisdom. Before there was anything, he asserts, there was Torah. So, too, teaches the Gospel of John in the Christian Bible: "In the beginning, was the Word, and the Word was with God" (1:1). But what kind of "word" was that? This primeval word could not have been a word as we understand words. After all, words are part of language, and language is a product of culture. This word existed before language, before culture, before humans were even created. This word was of divine language. The archetype Torah was written not in our language, but in a divine idiom. If so, what is its relationship to our Torah, the Torah in the synagogue ark?

Our Torah, written in human language, is but a facsimile of that archetype Torah, reworked so as to be accessible to human minds. In the language of later mysticism, the words of our Torah are but the garment in which the true, divine, archetypal Torah is clothed. Perhaps a more contemporary metaphor: the Torah is not text but hypertext. The words of the Torah are links to the true

Torah. They are not intrinsically meaningful, any more than "Google" is meaningful. Instead, they function as access points to the divine blueprint of the universe. Click on it, and we enter an entirely different world.

This revelation of a secret world of knowledge lying beneath the surface of the Torah text is an invitation to Kabbalah, the remarkable realm of Jewish mysticism. Mysticism begins with the intuition that there is a realm of reality that is more true and more real than everyday experience. The pursuit of mysticism offers a personal experience of that reality. *Kabbalah* literally means "the received tradition." It refers to the long tradition of mystical wisdom, imagination, and practice that developed in parallel to the normative forms of Judaism. Kabbalah offered access to a world of secret wisdom—the blueprints of Creation, and through that, into the inner life of God.

Like Maimonides, the mystics yearned to know God. But in sharp distinction to Maimonides, the mystics believed this knowledge was accessible neither by rationality nor by research. Divine wisdom was not intellectual. It was gained through other means— transmitted from master to student across the generations, or extracted from sacred texts by mystical interpretation, or revealed directly by an angel, the spirit of an ancient prophet or sage.

Because mysticism removes us from the realm of normal experience, it was deemed dangerous by tradition. The Rabbis of the Talmud set stern limits on the range of legitimate inquiry.

> Anyone who looks into these four things, it would have been better if he had not come into the world: what is above and what is below, what was before [Creation] and what will be after [the End].[13]

The world of experience ought to occupy us, they instructed. That is enough. Exploring what is above and what is below, what was before and what will be after, leads to heresy or insanity. But the human imagination cannot be so restricted. For certain human personalities, a "Do Not Enter" sign is an enticing invitation. And especially in moments of political and social upheaval, we look to the heavens to understand how the world works and why we suffer.

RESCUING THE PRINCESS

The same political instability that drove Maimonides out of Cordoba—the internecine conflicts among Moslem powers and the unrelenting Christian Reconquista—brought a flowering of Jewish mysticism to medieval Spain. And the same spiritual challenge that dominated his concern—confirming the truth of Judaism in a world of militant Christianity and Islam—inspired the mystic inquiry. In the thirteenth century, the Zohar, the greatest text of Jewish mysticism, appeared in Spain. A work of breathtaking imagination and astonishing images, it purports to come from Rabbi Shimon bar Yochai, a second-century Talmudic sage. Modern scholarship has demonstrated that it was authored largely by the Spanish mystic Moses de Leon and his circle.

The Zohar is premised on the idea that everything that happens below, in the world of our experience, reflects processes happening above, in the world of the Divine. This language of "below" and "above" are metaphors. The Zohar refers to "the experienced world without" and "the divine world within," or "the world of appearances" in contrast to "the world of truth." The Zohar is a meditation on religious symbols. It perceives our world as a symbol of the deeper, more real world of the Divine. The Zohar mystics sought to penetrate that divine world to understand the workings of our world and perhaps to find relief from their tribulations. To understand the upheavals of their time, they sought to glimpse the events at the beginning of time.

In the beginning was *Ein Sof,* literally, "The Infinite"—the Divine that cannot be known or conceived by the human mind. Mysteriously, there arose within *Ein Sof* the will to create the universe. From *Ein Sof* flowed ten streams of divine energy or projections of divine power, called *sefirot.* The concept of the *sefirot* is the key to the Zohar tradition. In the mystic imagination, the *sefirot* take on personalities, male and female characters, and specific roles in the creation and governance of the universe. As well, they function as clusters of symbols. The entire Torah can be read as an esoteric, coded message, deciphered by using the *sefirot* as a code key.

Ein Sof is beyond human understanding. The *sefirot* are the expressions of God within the comprehension of human beings. The fact of their multiplicity and the dynamic tensions among them means that God is no longer conceived as radically one. For the mystics, God is a committee, or an organism composed of parts functioning in harmony. Even more radical is the concept of the tenth of the *sefirot,* called *Malchut* or *Shechinah,* the felt presence of God in the world. The Hebrew noun *Shechinah,* literally "presence," occurs in the grammatical feminine, and so *Shechinah* is identified with the divine feminine. She is Queen, Bride, Princess, Mother.

None of this sounds like Judaism. The great twentieth-century scholar Gershom Scholem pointed out that in the mystic tradition, all the mythical images and themes so carefully weeded out of Judaism by the biblical tradition came roaring back to life.[14] In response to the austere rationalism of Maimonides, mysticism reveled in the creative play of religious imagination.

In the mystic myth, the world was intended to be a dynamic harmony among the *sefirot*—justice balanced by mercy, individuation by unity, masculine by feminine. But in the process of Creation, something went awry. A catastrophe occurred. An imbalance among the *sefirot* left the *sefirah* of *Din,* the power of individuation, untempered and unimpeded. As a result, *Malchut/Shechinah* became detached from the other *sefirot* and was exiled. The function of *Shechinah* was to gather the divine creative energy of all the *sefirot* and channel it into our world. With the exile of *Shechinah*, the channel became occluded. Our world lies bereft of its life-giving energy. The crisis of our world, therefore, reflects a crisis in the life of God—power divorced from compassion, justice from mercy, the masculine in God from the feminine. The exile and powerlessness suffered by the Jewish people is the earthly reflection of the catastrophic exile suffered by the loving element of God's being.

The cause of this cataclysm was Adam's original sin. But not the sin normally ascribed to him. Placed in the Garden, Adam was shown two trees—the Tree of Life and the Tree of Knowledge of Good and Evil. The two trees, according to the Zohar, were really one, growing from one trunk. The sin of Adam was not that he ate of a forbidden fruit, as Genesis indicates. The sin was that Adam separated the two trees, dividing knowledge from life, and ate from the Tree of Knowledge alone. Knowledge separated from life yields death. Adam's act destroyed the world of unity intended by God. Separation in the world below brought cataclysm in the world above. In the description of the thirteenth-century Spanish kabbalist Joseph ben Abraham Gikatila:

> At the beginning of Creation, the essence of the *Shechinah* dwelled in the lower regions, for the plan for Creation was to mirror the upper and lower worlds.... Each one was adorned from the other and each was filled with the other, and the channels and well-springs worked together perfectly, drawing from above to below as God filled what was below from above.... Then came Adam and sinned, ruining the system, blocking the channels, causing the water from the pools [or, the blessings] to cease. So the *Shechinah* fled. Thus the [world's] order unraveled. And *Shechinah* roamed like an itinerant from place to place.[15]

For the philosopher, evil is an intellectual problem to be explained away. But for popular religion and for the mystic, evil, especially in the form of human suffering, is a felt reality. The philosopher may explain evil as a deprivation, a gap in divine providence or benevolence. For the mystics, evil exists and is personified as a sinister force in the world, waiting to intrude at every moment. The Zohar perceives evil as the dark side of God's character—God's anger unchecked by God's mercy. Sin, understood as an individual's separation from the world's unity, elicits God's judgment and invites this insidious power into reality. Only the devotion of the faithful has the power to push back and vanquish this invasion. This is the heroic role of the religious Jew.

In the twelfth century, as the Jewish mystics of Spain were formulating their theories, the troubadour tradition arrived in Spain. The troubadours brought tales of knights and ladies, battles, and forlorn loves. They spread a culture of chivalry, the warrior's quest for honor and glory. The Zohar's mystic myth is a stirring tale of chivalry in symbolic form: the Princess has been kidnapped by forces of Evil and spirited away from her home and her intended. She lies hidden in a castle fortress somewhere in the wilderness, guarded by demons and dragons, waiting for rescue. Who shall save her, but the brave knight errant. And who is that knight? The devoted Jew. Powerless in the real world, the Jew gained heroic status in the mystic imagination. The fate of the world rested on his shoulders as he went to redeem the Princess. In the Zohar's imagination, it is the task of the human being to rescue God and restore God's unity.

What empowers the human to redeem God? What weapons does this knight carry into the battle? The human being is possessed of a soul, which is itself a projection of divine power, a reflection of the *sefirot*. The human soul has three parts: *nefesh*, the animal soul, its lowest part; *ruach*, the intellectual soul, its intermediate; and *neshamah*, the highest part of the soul, the connection with the worlds above. These three elements themselves originate and reflect the *sefirot*. Again, Gikatila:

> This *sefirah*, *Binah*, is called *Teshuvah* [Repentance or Return] because the *neshamot* emanate from this place, and the *ruchot* from [the *sefirah*] *Tiferet*, and the *nefashot* from the *sefirah* *Malchut* [*Shechinah*]. And they connect with one another until they merit attachment with the *sefirah Binah*. How does this work? The *nefesh* is connected to the *ruach*, and the *ruach* to the *neshamah*, and the *neshamah* is connected to the *sefirah Binah*. If the *Nefesh* sins ... she is cut off from *Ruach* ... and thus she has no way to ascend to the world to come.... If however she returns and betters her ways and repairs her pathways, then she returns [to connection] and then she is worthy of ascending.... This is the essence of *Teshuvah*.[16]

The human being carries a reflection of God within. Therefore, healing the breach in God and repairing the world begin by unifying the soul within. The process of redeeming the world begins with aligning the soul's animal, intellectual, and spiritual elements. The healing of God begins with healing the self.

The implements carried by the knight errant are ritual, prayer, and devotion. Outwardly, the mystic practices the same rites and rituals, celebrates the same holidays, observes the same religious laws as any other Jew. But inwardly, the intention is distinct. Inwardly, the rites become weapons in a desperate war against evil. They become tools in the redemption of the world.

According to the Zohar, to live as a devoted Jew is to participate in the life of God, for God's fate rests in the hands of the devoted. For Spanish Jews of the thirteenth century, buffeted by forces beyond their control, this offered a measure of dignity and purpose to life. Every ritual act carried the power to rescue the Divine. A powerful example of this is the Zohar's unique and startling explanation for the recitation of Judaism's signal statement of faith, *Shema Yisrael.*

> When Israel engages in the mystical unification of the *Shema* with a perfect will, a light emerges from the secret supernal world, and the light strikes the sparks of the blackness from within and splits up into seventy lights, and these seventy shine on the seventy branches of the Tree of Life [*Tiferet*]. This tree then exhales perfumes and spices, and all the trees in the Garden of Eden exhale perfumes, and praise their Master, for then the consort is adorned for entry into the chamber with her husband.[17]

The lost Princess, *Shechinah,* has been rescued from the clutches of evil by the brave knight errant. Riding home together, the knight sends word ahead to the Prince that they are returning. *Shema Yisrael* is that message. *Tiferet* is the *sefirah* representing the masculine powers of God. *Tiferet* prepares for the homecoming of his intended.

An astonishing feature of the Zohar tradition is its eroticism. Beyond its mythic images, the Zohar employs blatantly erotic language without embarrassment. The ultimate project of the Zohar's mysticism is unification, and there is no more emotionally powerful and evocative symbol of unification than sexual union.

Separated for some time now, the royal couple are nervous and reticent about their impending reunification and its consummation. Our prayer is intended to encourage them. There is no magic in the prayer itself, but there is great power in the perfect and pure intention we bring to the prayer. As the parts of the human soul align—*nefesh, ruach, neshamah*—the *sefirot* above align.

> All the supernal limbs are united together in a single desire and with a single will to be one, without any separation. Her

husband conceives the intention of bringing her to the chamber to be one with her, to unite with his consort. Therefore, we arouse her and say: *Shema Yisrael* (Hear, Israel, i.e., *Shechinah*): Prepare yourself. Your husband [*Tiferet*] comes to you in all his finery and is ready to meet you.

"Adonai our God, Adonai is One" [must be recited] in a single unification, with a single will, without any separation; for [then] all the limbs become one and enter into a single desire. When Israel says, "Adonai is One" we arouse the six extremities, these six extremities immediately become one and enter into a single desire. And the mystic symbol of this is the letter *vav*, a simple, single extension without any other attachment to it, but one on its own.[18]

"Israel" is one of the coded names for *Shechinah*. The statement *Shema Yisrael*, "Hear, O Israel," is directed at *Shechinah*, encouraging her to meet her Prince. The divine name *YHVH*, the tetragrammaton, is a code name for the *sefirah Tiferet*, the divine masculine. The next four words of the *Shema* are directed to encouraging him. Of the ten *sefirot*, the top three are considered beyond human experience. That leaves the bottom seven. The exile of *Shechinah* now leaves six. These six pour their energies into *Tiferet* in preparation for the union with *Shechinah*. This is symbolized in the six words of the *Shema Yisrael*. It is also symbolized by the six appendages of the male body—arms, legs, head, phallus—which must be aligned for physical intimacy. Finally, the sixth letter of the Hebrew alphabet is *vav*, which is written as a single, straight line, a symbol of unification and arousal.

Thus the consort prepares herself and adorns herself, and her ministers bring her to her husband, whispering in a soft voice, "Blessed is the name of God's glorious kingdom forever and ever." This blessing is said in a whisper, for this is the correct way to bring her to her husband. Happy are the people who know this and who order this celestial arrangement of faith.... When he is united above with the six extremities, she is likewise united below with six other extremities, so there is a unity above and a unity below, "Adonai shall be one and God's name one" (Zechariah 14:9).[19]

In the powerful imagination of the Zohar tradition, the unity of God is not a fact or a tenet of belief, but an aspiration. God has, in fact, become fragmented, broken. This is the ultimate cause of the world's suffering. Through acts of devotion, human beings heroically heal the fracture within the person of God, but only if that devotion is carried out with pure intention and perfect unity of soul. Then can the devoted knight errant complete the mission, defeat the forces of separation and evil, and unite the Prince with his lost Princess. Once united, the flow of divine energy and blessing into the world is restored. The devoted Jew is singularly responsible for mending the rupture within God and returning the flow of blessing into the world.

But even here, the Zohar tradition was relatively modest in its ambition. Characteristic of medieval Judaism, the repair is affected only in the devotional life of the mystic, not in the politics of the world. Moreover, the restoration is a momentary and temporary reprieve, not a permanent fix. Only in the next iteration of the Kabbalah would the mystics muster the chutzpah to imagine themselves capable of achieving the final and complete redemption of the world.

HEALING THE COSMOS

Since the destruction of the Temple in 70 CE, Jews have suffered persecution in many places and expulsion from many lands. But none matched the impact of the expulsion of Jews from Spain in

1492. Culminating seven hundred years of Jewish life in Spain, the experience of expulsion contrasted sharply with the heights of cultural creativity and social integration of Spanish Jews. The expulsion was followed by a deep awareness of exile as the persistent feature of Jewish existence. The unredeemed state of the world became a painfully felt reality. So catastrophic was the experience that it generated a wave of apocalyptic speculation. The statesman and scholar Don Isaac Abarvenel declared it the "birth pangs of the Messiah" and predicted the Messiah would arrive in 1503. The kabbalist Abraham ben Eliezer Ha-Levi foretold the Messiah's arrival in 1524. When no redemption came, the communities of Spanish exiles turned to spiritual realms to seek an answer and a remedy for their plight.

In 1516, the Ottoman Empire conquered Palestine from the Mamluks and welcomed Jewish immigration to the Holy Land. The town of Safed became a center for trade in textiles and soon attracted an influx of Spanish refugees. Among them were the leading lights of Jewish mysticism. In the clear, cool air of the Northern Galilee, the mystics formed a community. For the first time in Jewish history, mysticism moved from a private and secret pursuit to a collective enterprise shared by an entire community.

As happens in Jewish history, catastrophe was followed by surge of collective genius gathered to define a response. The destruction of the Temple generated the first generations of the Mishnaic Rabbis—Yochanan ben Zakkai, Rabbi Eliezer, Rabbi Yehoshua, Rabbi Akiba, and their students. So, too, the expulsion of Spain brought together in one place the lights of Kabbalah—Joseph Karo, Moshe Cordovero, Shlomo Ha-Levi Alkabetz, Eliezer Azikri, and the greatest of them all, Isaac Luria, known as the Ari, the divine Rabbi Yitzchak.

Luria is the undisputed champion of chutzpah in Jewish history, though he never wrote a book or published a monograph, he lived in total obscurity up until the last two and a half years of his life. Like Mozart, he died very young, but in a very short career, he changed the way we experience the world. He introduced a new Jewish narrative and a revolutionary religious vocabulary. And he exalted the vision of human capacity far above any previous conception in Jewish history.

Luria was born in 1534 in Jerusalem. His father came from Germany to partake in the freedom promised by the Ottomans. His mother was of Sephardic origin. He received a traditional Jewish education and was recognized early as a scholar of Jewish law. In his early youth, his father died, and his mother took the family to Cairo to live with her brother. Luria learned with the leading rabbis of the community, married the daughter of his teacher, and began a career as a spice merchant. In his mid-twenties, Luria retired to a life of solitude on a small island in the Nile, where he entered into the life of contemplative mysticism. He emerged in 1570, visited Jerusalem, and then joined the mystical fellowship of Safed. In very short order, Luria gathered a powerful following, promulgated a revolutionary kabbalistic myth with a new set of mystical practices and rites, and then died suddenly in 1572 at the age of thirty-eight. His teachings are recorded in the writings of his students, principally Hayim Vital and Joseph ibn Tabul.

Lurianic Kabbalah is a gigantic baroque cathedral of myth, symbols, wordplays, rites, and practices. At its heart, Luria succeeded in turning the attention of Jewish mysticism from the beginning of time to the end of time. He married Kabbalah to messianism, infusing his followers with the confidence that they could bring redemption to the world. No longer was the Messiah's arrival solely in the hands of God. Redemption will come only if the devout and dedicated work for it. We Jews, living on history's periphery, may appear inconsequential. In fact, we are the leading actors in the divine drama of redemption. We stand on a cosmic stage performing the part of world redeemers. Nothing we do in the course of life is insignificant in this process. Every act, even the most mundane conduct of ordinary life, has the power to hasten the end of exile and return the world to Eden.

The Lurianic myth is inordinately complex. It can be summarized basically into three movements: *tzimtzum*, "withdrawal"; *shevirat ha-keilim*, "breaking of the vessels"; and *tikkun*, "repair."

TZIMTZUM: MAKING ROOM FOR FREEDOM AND RESPONSIBILITY

Luria taught:

> Before the emanation of any of the emanated entities, the divine light completely suffused all of existence, and there was no free space, no empty vacuum whatsoever. Rather, everything was filled with the undifferentiated light of *Ein Sof*. There was neither beginning nor end, but everything consisted of the one simple undifferentiated light, called *Ein Sof*.[20]

"In the beginning, God …"—there was only God. And God's fullness crowds out any other creation. For Creation to happen, God needed to make space. *Tzimtzum* refers to the withdrawal of God from a zone, a pulling back, to accommodate the phenomenal universe. Prior to emanation, the pouring of divine reality into the world, there had to be a gesture of divine retraction, just as inhaling precedes exhaling.

> When *Ein Sof* determined to create its world and to issue forth the world of emanated entities, to bring to light the fullness of God's energies, names and qualities, this being the reason for the creation of the world … *Ein Sof* then withdrew itself from its centermost point, the center of its light, and this light retreated from the center to the sides, and thus there remained a free space, an empty vacuum.[21]

As a metaphysical idea and a description of the psychology of creativity, *tzimtzum* is a remarkably suggestive concept. As a moral construct, *tzimtzum* reconciles a belief in an omnipotent God with an equally firm belief in the moral freedom of human beings. We are free and responsible actors in the world because God granted that freedom by withdrawing to make room for us.

SHEVIRAT HA-KEILIM: BROKEN VESSELS, DIVINE SPARKS

Into the empty space, God poured being. This being massed within the space, then separated into four worlds, or stages of the creative process: Emanation, Creation, Formation, Actualization. Through these worlds, God then sent one beam of light. This beam refracted into the ten *sefirot*. As the ten beams arrived in the lower worlds, they required vessels to contain them. The vessels formed themselves from the mass. But that mass held a surplus of *Din*, the divine attribute of Judgment, or individuation. The vessels were imperfect and could not contain the divine light entering reality. They exploded. The world, taught Luria, began in *shevirat ha-keilim*, a big bang. The *kelipot*, or shards of these broken vessels, formed our material world. Each shard is filled with a spark of the divine light. That spark yearns to be raised and reunited with its source in the Divine. Thus, an element of God lives in exile, just as we do. And the suffering we experience in our exile is an expression of the divine rupture that brought our world into being.

TIKKUN: LIBERATING THE LIGHT, REPAIRING THE WORLD

When the original divine light entered the world, it formed a human configuration, *Adam Kadmon* (primordial man). After the crisis of the vessels' explosion, God formed the human being along the same configuration with the express purpose of gathering and rescuing the scattered sparks of divinity. We are formed in the con-figuration of the universe itself; therefore, we possess the ability to affect *tikkun ha-olam*, the repair of the universe. With the creation of the human being, the universe began to heal. Had Adam and Eve behaved as they were instructed, the process of repair would have been complete by the afternoon of the first Sabbath. But the sin of Adam and Eve caused a regression, bringing everything crashing down once again. And now it is the perennial task of their descendants to complete the work of *tikkun,* world repair.

There is divine light scattered throughout the world, taught Luria. The project of *tikkun,* liberating that light trapped in the material world, constitutes the purpose of human existence. The special career of the Jewish people is to use the exquisite tools of Torah and its commandments in the service of *tikkun.* The exile and diffusion of the Jewish nation is an essential part of this drama.

> This is the secret why Israel is fated to be enslaved by all the Gentiles of the world: In order that it may uplift those sparks which have fallen among them.... And therefore it was neces-sary that Israel be scattered to the four winds in order to lift everything up.[22]

Exile is no longer punishment or penance. Israel is the secret agent of God tasked with locating the fallen divine light in the life of the world and returning it upward. For Luria, like the Zohar before him, *tikkun* was accomplished not by action in the political world, but by the practices of contemplative devotion.

Luria's Kabbalah offered his followers a leading role in the divine drama of world redemption. The stage for this drama is the everyday life, ritual as well as profane, of the ordinary Jew. No act of life was deemed mundane. Every act, from morning until night, was envisioned as a significant moment in the cosmic struggle between brokenness and repair, good and evil, exile and redemption. Every human deed, no matter how routine and ordinary, was perceived as an opportunity for *tikkun*. The way a meal is taken, how money is handled, how one dresses in the morning or retires to sleep at night, even, and most especially, sexual relations between husband and wife, were carefully scripted to ensure their comportment contributed to the project of world redemption.

Luria and his followers were meticulous in their observance of Jewish traditional practices. But each of those practices received a new thick overlay of symbolic significance. For Luria, intention in the performance of a ritual act carried supreme significance.

> [God's will] can only be achieved by one who knows the [kab-balistic] intention of prayer and the mitzvot, and who [medi-tatively] intends to mend the upper worlds, and to unite the name of the Holy One of blessing, blessed by God [the *sefirah Tiferet*] with *Shechinah*. And his intention should have noth-ing to do with receiving reward in this world, nor even for the benefit in the world to come.... Even in connection with the study of Torah, do not think that it is for the purpose of learn-ing its content, but do so ... in order to unite the Holy One of blessing, with *Shechinah*.[23]

Ritual observances were accompanied by elaborate *kavanot*, meditations, designed to focus the mind and heart on the unique redemptive quality of the ritual.

Because the world's original design designated the first Sabbath to be the day when Adam would complete the task of res-toration, Luria's circle created elaborate rituals integrating every moment of the Sabbath into the divine drama. Most familiar is the addition of *Kabbalat Shabbat*, a service of psalms and hymns, to the traditional evening prayers on Friday night. But that just initiates the kabbalist's Sabbath observance. Hayim Vital recounts his teacher's instructions for the next steps. Upon returning home from evening prayers in the synagogue, the Jewish man gathers his family with song and joy.

> For such an individual may be compared to a bridegroom who greets the bride with tremendous happiness and warmth. If your mother is still living, go and kiss her hands. The esoteric significance of this is that in a similar way [the lower *sefirot*] kisses the hand of his mother [the *sefirah Binah*, mother of all being] each Sabbath night.... Then circle the table once in silence, from the right side [invoking the presence of the *sefirah Chesed*, or kindness]. Following this, take in your hands two bundles of myrtles and encircle the table once again in silence.... The two bundles signify [the upper or masculine *sefirot* and the separated feminine *Shechinah*], which are united [on Sabbath].[24]

Twelve loaves of challah graced Luria's table, in remembrance of the Temple's showbread. Each ritual of the Sabbath table had a special role in reuniting the disparate parts of the Divine with their source. At midnight, Luria's followers arose to share intimacy with their wives, but always focusing on the reunification of the divine masculine and feminine. Every moment of Shabbat was infused with this intention and level of intensity. At its end, the close of Shabbat was delayed, extending the day long into the night, on the chance that this moment might see the prophet Elijah arriving to announce the coming of Messiah.

Most significantly, Luria taught his followers to embrace their role in the drama of cosmic redemption with joy. Melancholy was not permitted in his circle. Luria's magical rites could not alter the material conditions of the Jewish people. Instead, he offered them a role in the divine drama of cosmic redemption. He endowed them with the dignity of human beings empowered and responsible to take part in the great struggle to heal the Divine and redeem the world. He could not bring Eden into the world. But he could guide them to find Eden within. Luria's invitation to participate in the life of God was enough to repel the bitterness of exile suffered by a broken people and restore the special sense of mission embraced by the Jewish people. As the prophet taught, "Not by might, not by power, but by My spirit—said Adonai of Hosts" (Zechariah 4:6).

Chapter Six

LIKE A FIDDLER
ON THE ROOF

A fiddler on the roof.... Sounds crazy, no? But here, in our little village of Anatevka, you might say every one of us is a fiddler on the roof trying to scratch out a pleasant, simple tune without breaking his neck. It isn't easy. You may ask, why do we stay up there if it's so dangerous? Well, we stay because Anatevka is our home. And how do we keep our balance? That I can tell you in one word! Tradition!... And because of our traditions, every one of us knows who he is and what God expects him to do. (*Fiddler on the Roof*, act 1, scene 1)

Every American Jew knows the opening lines of *Fiddler on the Roof*. *Fiddler* has become the American Jewish myth of origin, the narrative we would like to believe about our beginnings. Like liturgy, it is recited at every special moment of communal gathering. What Jewish wedding is complete without a rendition of "Sunrise, Sunset"?

Fiddler celebrates the world of Tevye, a character created by the Yiddish author Sholem Aleichem. Tevye was a poor milkman struggling with the life of a Russian Jewish peasant at the turn of the twentieth century. From every objective standpoint, his life was miserable but for his sweet and innocent faith in a God who is part of the family. Tevye is our imaginary collective ancestor, the wise and loving great-grandfather we would all wish for. And Anatevka, his village, is the place we all wish we came from—a world of uncomplicated truth and simple meaning, where everyone knows "who he is and what God expects him to do." Anatevka offers the reassurance that once upon a time, in a land far away, we knew lives of devotion, purity, and purpose. Life was lived in accord with eternal truths and timeless wisdom. How was this possible? "That I can tell you in one word," Tevye declares in the show's opening blockbuster: "Tradition!"

American Jews flocked to *Fiddler* for a sweet taste of the world of tradition. The irony is that *Fiddler on the Roof* is not about tradition. *Fiddler* is about the radical changes that destroyed the world of tradition. In that sense, it really is the story of our origins as modern Jews and the birth of the complicated identities we inhabit.

The lives of three of Tevye's daughters drive the drama. Each of these lives describes one element of the revolution that overturned Tevye's world. Daughters of a poor, undistinguished family, Tevye's girls have little capital in the marriage market. Their uncertain future rests in the hands of the all-knowing Yenta the Matchmaker. So there is great rejoicing when Yenta finally arrives to share wonderful news—the eldest daughter, Tzeitel, has been chosen to wed the wealthy butcher Lazar Wolf. Yes, Lazar Wolf is an older man, a widower, and more than occasionally he drinks and gets violent, but a match with Lazar Wolf the butcher promises a life of comfort for a girl from a poor family. The family is ecstatic—until the moment Tzeitel announces that she refuses the match. Instead of Lazar Wolf, Tzeitel has pledged herself to marry her childhood companion, the tailor Motel Kamzoil. Tevye is astonished. In vain he protests: "If I say you will, you will!"

How did Tzeitel suddenly gain the right to choose her own husband? What happened to respect for parents and tradition?

And why would she give up a match with the wealthy Lazar Wolf to marry a poor, starving, unaccomplished tailor? Because, Tzeitel confesses, I love him. In this confession, Tzeitel ignites the revolution we call modernity.

THE BIRTH OF THE CHOOSING SELF

The world of tradition wrote one's life script long before you were born. Every fact of personal life, even the most intimate, was prescribed by family and community custom. In the traditional world, there was no sense of an independent self. Self was totally embedded in community and family. There were no choices to be made. There were no alternatives. Life was guided from beginning to end by the defining authority of tradition. Life was not about the pursuit of personal happiness or satisfaction or love. Faithfully fulfilling the dictates of tradition was all that mattered.

Tzeitel's announcement shatters this world. With her announcement, something new is born into the world—the choosing self. Tzeitel's rebellion removes the locus of authority from family, community, and tradition and relocates it to the individual. Romantic love is an apt symbol of this revolution, for the veneration of romantic love is the triumph of personal autonomy. Tzeitel represents the unencumbered, autonomous self—the independent, emotional, psychological, subjective self, rising to overcome the power of external authority. Tzeitel embodies the freedom we claim as individuals to choose our own fate, choose the course of our lives, choose our own values. This assertion of personal freedom dissolves the world of unquestioned, unchallenged tradition. With Tzeitel's announcement, Tevye begins to see his world disintegrate. Could Judaism survive a marriage to modern individualism? What becomes of the authority of tradition when the pursuit of personal happiness is elevated as life's highest value?

And Tevye doesn't have it any easier with his other daughters. Hodel, the second daughter, falls in love with Perchik, the revolutionary running from the czar's police. In a tearful scene, she leaves behind her family to follow him into exile in Siberia.

Medieval Judaism removed the Jewish people from history. It held that God was the principal actor in history. We humans are but bystanders, spectators to the unfolding of the divine plan. It is our lot to wait, to live pious lives and to pray for God's redemption. By the late nineteenth century, Jews had had enough waiting. They deemed the mysticism and devotional exercises of their medieval ancestors to be magical thinking—elaborate expressions of passivity and impotence. They'd had enough of powerlessness. Socialism, communism, bolshevism, capitalism, Zionism, all attracted the energies of younger Jews. Each of these movements offered Jews a vision of freedom to shape the conditions of their own existence. They provided an escape from the indignity of feeble weakness. They offered an alternative to the historical role of Jew as perpetual victim. They envisioned a new Jew, possessed of the dignity of self-reliance and strength. And they dreamed of the power to bring redemption now, in this world.

Hodel's tearful departure from home to follow her lover is an act of liberation from the exile that Jews had accepted for eighteen centuries. She represents modernity's suspension of the traditional theory of history—the theory that sustained the Jewish people through the Middle Ages—and its replacement with a modern sense of empowerment and collective responsibility. Eventually, Hodel's departure would bring the Jewish people home to the Land of Israel and to sovereignty. It would bring them to the heights of American prosperity and power. It would place Jews in the leadership of great movements of social revolution. But it also destroys another pillar of Tevye's secure world. Would Judaism survive a marriage to modern social activism? Could it withstand the dissolution of its traditional ideological defenses?

Finally, there was Chava. She was the shy girl whose nose was always in a book. Books were kept in the village library, which was adjacent to the church. And there she met and fell in love with Fyedka, a Russian boy who shared her love of books.

For most of the Middle Ages, Jewish cultural life was insular. With notable exceptions, such as Maimonides, Jews lived in a cognitive ghetto. In matters of faith and philosophy, they talked only with other Jews. The truth claims of Judaism were never tested outside the community's internal conversation. When civil emancipation released Jews from the walls of the physical ghetto, Jews were liberated into a world of new ideas. Modern sciences and philosophies came to challenge the truth of Jewish tradition. Hume's empiricism denied the existence of miracles. Copernicus evicted us from the center of God's universe. Darwin affirmed that we are animals—highly advanced primates with unusually large brains. Freud posited that all we create and dream are sublimations of sexual and aggressive drives. Durkheim discovered that every tribe asserts its prerogative as God's chosen people. Marx saw religion as part of the oppressive infrastructure serving the interests of the rich and the powerful. The modern, scientific study of ancient civilizations cast doubt on the integrity of the biblical text and its divine authorship. Modernity challenged the unquestioned faith in a present and loving God. The picture of the world that Tevye took for granted—the map that helped him navigate life—dissolved in the facts and philosophies of Chava's books.

Teyve could dance at Tzeitel's wedding to Motel Kamzoil. Judaism married to individualism might still bend back toward a life resembling tradition. And Tevye could bless Hodel on her way to join Perchik. Judaism married to social idealism was still familiar. Hodel's revolutionary spirit took her away from the family but in pursuit of Jewish dreams of redemption. But Teyve could not accept Chava's love of Fyedka. "Marrying out"—marrying a stranger from outside the culture, as well as marrying Judaism to foreign cultures and strange faiths—was a choice he could not abide. In Tevye's eyes, Chava's choice was a deliberate rejection of family and tradition because it irreversibly overturned the truths that shaped his life. And this, Tevye believed, ended his world even more decisively than the pogroms that destroyed his village.

American Jews packed theaters across North America to revel in *Fiddler on the Roof*. They came to taste, if for just an evening, the sweetness of their ancestors' simple faith, the security of their firm tradition, the truth of their folk wisdom. For twentieth-century American Jews, *Fiddler* offered a momentary visit to an imagined paradise, an Eden of tradition. But even as they left the theater singing the songs, perhaps they noticed that in the end, *Fiddler* does not leave us in that Eden. It is the story of our exile. Tevye's daughters rejected tradition and chose freedom instead. They tasted the forbidden fruits of modernity and gained autonomy, power, and knowledge. The taste of this new freedom was exhilarating. It offered so many new possibilities, but at the cost of the simple, secure world of tradition. As Tevye understood so rightly, "Without our traditions, our lives would be as shaky as ... as a fiddler on the roof!"

The deeper irony is that those same Jews who wept with nostalgia at *Fiddler* represent the greatest success story in the history of American modernity. As they hummed "If I Were a Rich Man," American Jews saw their children live out Tevye's dreams of wealth and influence. *Fiddler* opened on Broadway in 1964, just as the majority of American Jews were reaching their third generation in America. In those three generations, American Jews rose to the very top of the American socioeconomic pyramid, challenging the prerogatives of those who had been here for centuries. No ethnic group acculturated into America as quickly and efficiently as the descendants of Eastern European Jews. Modernity has been good to American Jews, and American Jews have been good at modernity.

Sholem Aleichem was a keen observer of modernity and a cogent critic of its problems. In his stories of Teyve's daughters, he reflected on modernity's blessings and discerned the challenges and dilemmas within those blessings. Because Jews were so successful at assimilating modernity, we are modernity's very best test case. At the heart of *Fiddler* is the question, Can Judaism survive in modernity? But even more—in Tevye's struggle, Sholem Aleichem asks a much broader question: Can humanity survive modernity? Tradition may have been stifling, but is this modernity a home we can inhabit? Because these questions were shared by peoples and cultures well beyond the Jewish community, *Fiddler* became a hit worldwide. *Fiddler* is cherished not only out of sentimentality, but also because, like Sholem Aleichem, so many of us in so many places intuit that amid the blessings of our modernity, something important is amiss.

Tzeitel, Hodel, and Chava asserted their freedom to choose, act, and think as independent individuals. Modernity prizes these qualities of independence, individualism, and most of all, freedom. But the freedom offered by modernity is incomplete. Modernity liberated the individual from the constraints of tradition and custom. It offers no vision of what to do with that freedom, how that freedom ought to be exercised, to what ends it should be invested. Modernity offers "freedom from," but not "freedom to." Because of his tradition, Tevye embraced a set of eternal truths and purposes that lent his life significance and his struggles meaning. Modernity undermines those purposes and the truths they are built on. But more, modernity undermines the very possibility of purpose and meaning in human life. Paradoxically, it diminishes freedom at the same time as it purports to liberate us. Each gesture of modernity captured in *Fiddler* betrays this paradox.

FREEDOM WITHOUT COMMUNITY

Tzeitel represents the individual's freedom of choice. This freedom to choose the pathway of one's own life, to make up one's own mind, to determine one's own values, is modernity's cornerstone. We value this freedom as sacred. We charge our children to think for themselves, stand up for what they believe in, assert their individuality, express themselves. Adulthood in modernity is defined as moral autonomy. Maturity arrives the day we can figure out by ourselves what is right and wrong and assume responsibility for our choices. But how are we to know what is right and wrong? Liberated from the authority of family and tradition, we surrendered our unquestioned adherence to tradition's values. On what basis do we make choices now? We claim the right to choose our own values. But how do we choose values if it is by values that we make choices?

Acknowledging no authority outside the choosing self, we turn our individual freedom of choice into our highest value. The sociologists call this "the sovereign self." No authority is ever placed above the self. Any commitment that encumbers the self, placing claims on the self, is perceived as diminishing personal freedom, and therefore diminishing the self. Preserving freedom at all costs becomes our mission. Inasmuch as any particular choice involves closing off options, the choosing self comes to resist entering into any relationship, committing to any cause, connecting to any binding obligation.

The greatest American cultural icons embody this individualist idea of freedom. We revere those who strike out on their own, break the rules, cut ties that bind, blaze their own way down the road less traveled: the explorer, the pioneer, the rebel, the maverick, the entrepreneur. The great nineteenth-century American thinker Ralph Waldo Emerson wrote the celebrated essay "Self Reliance," while his friend Henry David Thoreau sat alone by Walden Pond.

Relationships, community, and family come with claims and commitments. Our mythic heroes—historical and fictional—are loners: Daniel Boone, Amelia Earhart, Steve Jobs, the Lone Ranger, Superman, Shane, Dirty Harry, Han Solo. Relationships impinge on our freedom. They limit our choices. They evoke guilt and social claustrophobia. Cole Porter put this uniquely American spirit into popular song:

> *Let me be by myself in the evenin' breeze*
> *And listen to the murmur of the cottonwood trees*
> *Send me off forever but I ask you please*
> *Don't fence me in.*

Harvard sociologist Robert Putnam discovered a curious anomaly some years ago. More Americans go bowling than ever before. But many fewer bowl in organized leagues. More and more of us bowl alone, Putnam concluded.[1] He expanded his research and discovered that Americans have backed away from many of their associations: membership in PTA has declined dramatically, as has affiliation with civic clubs, lodges, community political organizations, neighborhood groups, churches and synagogues, municipal leagues, and ethnic associations. All have dropped precipitously over the past decades. The fabric of community has grown thin and frayed as we have lost what he calls our "social capital"—that set of associations and social connections that bind us into a coherent community.

When the sovereign self does enter into relationships, even the most personal relationships, it is in the guise of the consumer. As consumer, the sovereign self controls the transaction and can sever the connection at any time. The demands of the relationship can be negotiated. The relationship remains a "limited liability partnership." The novelist Henry James once said, in a wonderfully suggestive phrase, that America is "a hotel civilization." A hotel is a place we might sleep and eat, but we don't live there. We don't set down roots there. It's not ours. In a hotel, we never fully unpack. In a hotel, we can leave a mess, and someone comes in the middle of the day (someone you don't know) to straighten and clean up. In a hotel, we don't care who lives next door or across the hall. Their affairs are none of our business. We'll just check out and move on tomorrow. But who can live an entire life in a hotel?

We human beings gain a sense of purpose in life by attaching ourselves to causes bigger and grander than our own private concerns. We gain a sense of significance in narratives larger than our own lives. We gain meaning by serving eternal values. We gain identity by involving ourselves in relationships of love, friendship, collegiality, and community. The very freedom won by Tzeitel subverts these sensibilities, leaving us bereft and filled with nostalgic longing for Tevye's simple faith. Tzeitel's rebellion produces free but lonely selves, disconnected from the sources of life's meaning.

POWER WITHOUT PURPOSE

Hodel represents modernity's empowerment of human beings to assert control over history. Given the centuries of Jewish suffering and the indignity of Jewish passivity, this empowerment is certainly a blessing. There is a reason why Jews get teary-eyed at the strains of "Hatikvah," the fluttering of an Israeli flag, and photos of Israeli fighter planes flying over Auschwitz. The assertion of Jewish power is an assertion of the triumph of life over death. But this, too, is no pure blessing.

As long as Jews believed that God was history's actor and agent, they believed in the coming of the Messiah. No matter how brutal their experiences in history, they maintained faith that the end of history would bring redemption and salvation. Traditions abounded with visions of the nature of this end-time, including resurrection of the dead, rebuilding of the Temple in Jerusalem, the ingathering of all Jews, and a world of peace and tranquility. These fantasies sustained generations of Jews through the ordeals of exile, persecution, and humiliation. But they came with a price—the promise to remain powerless in history. In return for the promise of God's redemption, the Jewish people surrendered all claims to political power. Spiritual power became the source of Jewish life force. Politically, we pledged to remain passive and wait for God's chosen moment.

The twentieth century saw an explosion of Jewish revolutionary movements, which rejected the tradition's theology of passivity and sought to reclaim Jewish political power. Hodel and Perchik represent these movements. In reclaiming power, the revolutionaries displaced God from the central role of history actor. Zionism and Jewish social activism rebelled against traditional Judaism. They envisioned a redeemed world and sought power to realize that vision. But while they rejected the Jewish belief in the Messiah, they embraced the substance of the traditional Jewish messianic vision. The Zionists, after all, sought to return to the ancestral homeland and the language of the Bible and embraced a dream to build a perfected society.

Modernity offered the Jewish people the gifts of power. In 1897, Theodor Herzl convened the first Zionist Congress, gathering Jews from around the world to begin the political process that would return the Jewish people to sovereignty for the first time in 1,800 years. The power of sovereignty, Herzl promised, would solve "the Jewish problem." It would erase the anti-Semitism that plagued Jews in every corner of the world. Sovereignty, imagined other Zionist leaders, would bring a rebirth of the Jewish people with restored self-respect and national dignity. In the back of that first Zionist Congress sat a wise curmudgeon. Asher Zvi Ginsburg, writing under the pen name Ahad Ha-Am, also celebrated Jewish sovereignty, but he wondered aloud about the unforeseen dangers that attended the return of Jews to power. Responding to Theodor Herzl's stirring vision of a Jewish state, the wise curmudgeon Ahad Ha-Am sounded a cautionary note:

> A political ideal which is not grounded in our national culture is apt to seduce us from loyalty to our own inner spirit and to beget in us a tendency to find the path of glory in the attainment of material power and political domination, thus breaking the thread that unites us with the past and undermines our historical foundation.[2]

Power has a way of becoming an end and a value in itself, distracting its adherents from all other purposes. Hypnotized by the accouterments of our newly found power, warned Ahad Ha-Am, we are apt to neglect the larger tasks of cultural renaissance and national renewal and lose the essence of our cultural identity. Powerless for so long, we will come to worship power, bow before its symbols, and forget the dreams that sustained and defined us for so long. Power will become our god, and our visions of a redeemed world will be abandoned. We may yet gain power and all its blessings, but lose ourselves in the process.

WORLDLY WITHOUT WISDOM

Chava represents the opening of the Jewish mind. After centuries of isolation, Jews could once again swim in the vast sea of human culture. They quickly became its most enthusiastic mariners. Many believed that Jewish culture had grown stagnant and stale from its isolation. Ahad Ha-Am observed, "The people of the book have become a slave of the book."[3] Just as the Jews need to be liberated from their ghettos, he argued, Judaism must be liberated. As Judaism reentered world culture, he predicted, engaging the arts and philosophies of the world, it would enjoy a cultural renaissance. But this blessing, too, comes with a paradox.

Bar and bat mitzvah may be our formal religious rites marking coming of age, but the real rite of adulthood is when the child leaves home for college. Almost 90 percent of American Jewish youngsters are packed off to university. Chava's dreams are fulfilled in the contemporary American university. Consider that concept—"university"—an institution offering entry into the vast universe of cultures, sciences, arts, and ideas. The typical university academic catalog is breathtaking in the breadth, variety, and ingenuity of its opportunities. Young people set off to university filled with all their parents' values, aspirations, and ideals. But when they return home, they are very different. University life has a way of washing youngsters clean of all their parents' enculturation. The child sports a new hairstyle, perhaps a new piercing or tattoo, a new style of eating, new politics, new religious ideas, new personal values. Parents' values and commitments are dismissed as hopelessly unenlightened, primitive, even immoral.

In the lofty world of the university, all cultures are celebrated, and all narratives are embraced. All are valued equally. None is right or wrong, good or evil, true or false. The university is truly the world of the universal. From that precipice, all truths are relative, none is privileged. The view from that exalted perspective is exhilarating. How could any parent's simple wisdom compare? Confronted with familial values, the young university scholar proclaims, "That's just your opinion!"

The university evokes its own value system. Its ultimate value is its very openness. Tolerance is sacred. To be "judgmental" is sinful. Those who assert that one system of values, cultural perspective, or way of life is superior to others are summarily rejected. Embracing a particularism over the university's culture of universalism is heresy. But what works as an operational philosophy of inquiry in the setting of the university cannot be easily transplanted into the world of real life. How does one live life without making judgments and choices?

The paradox of pure universalism escapes the vociferous college freshman. If all values, truths, and cultures are equal, and none is privileged, then how does one choose from among them? If there is no standpoint or standard from which to evaluate ethics, life choices, or styles of living, then how does one form an identity, a point of view, an opinion? Total openness forestalls all choices, precludes all commitments, until ultimately it subverts all identity. It is no wonder that university life is notorious for its extreme moral license. When anything goes, it is said, everything goes.

"DO YOU LOVE ME?"

Tevye: Golde, do you love me?
Golde: Do I what?
    T: Do you love me?

    G: Do I love you?
        With our daughters getting married,
        And this trouble in the town,
        You're upset, you're worn out, go inside, go lie
        down. Maybe it's indigestion.

    T: Golde, I'm asking you a question—
        Do you love me?
    G: You're a fool!
    T: I know—but do you love me?

The most touching moment of the play comes near the end of *Fiddler*'s second act. Tevye and Golde are suddenly alone, and he poses the simplest and most startling question: Do you love me? She does not understand the question. A child of tradition, Golde has done all that tradition asks of her as a wife and mother; she has fulfilled her role, met her obligation.

G: Do I love you?
   For twenty-five years I've washed your clothes,
   Cooked your meals, cleaned your house,
   Given you children, milked the cow,
   After twenty-five years,
   Why talk about love right now?

Right now is the time to ask. Tradition has waned. Without the tradition's obligation forcing us together, he wonders, do you love me? Absent tradition's sense of inevitability, would you choose me? And not just Tevye. Once upon a time, all our truths and values and patterns of life were bequeathed to us by tradition. We had no choices. But modernity has disabled the power of tradition and custom to demand anything of us. What values we hold today are the values we have chosen. We have chosen to embrace our vision of the world. In this confusing new world, the voice of the ancient Jewish tradition asks the modern Jew, Do you love me? Given the universe of your choices and your newfound freedom, do you choose me?

T: Golde, the first time I met you was on our wedding
   day. I was scared.
G: I was shy.
T: I was nervous.
G: So was I.
T: But my father and my mother said we'd learn to
   love each other and now I'm asking, Golde, do you
   love me?
G: I'm your wife!
T: I know—but do you love me?

In throwing off the authority of tradition and asserting their freedom, Tzeitel, Hodel, and Chava brought a new world into being.

But this world is incomplete. Modernity empowers the human being. It celebrates the freedom of the self. But it offers no wisdom on how this freedom should be used. It offers no transcendent purposes that might lend life meaning. Instead, it undermines the very idea of transcendent purpose, leaving Tzeitel's grandchildren bereft. They search for life's meaning, but they haven't the tools to find it.

It would seem that in celebrating human freedom, modernity has embraced a kind of chutzpah. The empowerment of the human being, as we have seen, is what chutzpah was always about. But not all that it was about. Chutzpah was always more than freedom. Abraham left home not only to become great and to achieve a great name. Abraham's charge was to "be a blessing" (Genesis 12:2). Jewish tradition celebrated human possibilities, but toward the end of achieving a larger vision of a world of oneness. Chutzpah was not about selfhood for its own sake, but about bringing Eden into reality. The self celebrated by modernity is too small. The ideal of chutzpah held up a self that expanded to include the world. In doing so, chutzpah lent meaning and purpose to human existence. Eden was not ultimately about freedom. Eden is about oneness. Missing from modernity is that critical element within chutzpah.

This message was conveyed by a group of great Jewish thinkers writing in the twentieth century. Ostensibly, they sought to interpret Judaism to a modern, secular, assimilated Jewish community. In this, they attempted to rescue Judaism from modernity. But in doing so, they uncovered a pathway toward a much greater goal—rescuing modernity from itself. These thinkers grasped the paradox of modernity: in collapsing the world into the self and its freedom, modernity compromises the self and destroys that freedom. They deployed the conceptual tools of Judaism to save modernity. They brought chutzpah into the modern world.

MARTIN BUBER: ALL REAL LIFE IS MEETING

Tzeitel's rebellion may have ignited modernity for Jews, but for Western civilization, modernity began in the seventeenth century with the thinking of the French philosopher René Descartes. Descartes asked a simple scientific question: What can I know for certain? In a remarkable thought experiment, duplicated annually by young philosophy students, Descartes cast aside all that tradition and custom had taught, for none of that could be demonstrated with certainty. He doubted everything his senses told him, for senses can be fooled. He cleansed his mind of every preconceived idea and pattern of thought, until he arrived at the realization that all he knew for certain was his own doubt. But that was enough. "I think, therefore I am," Descartes famously concluded.

It somehow escaped Descartes that he was thinking in Latin, a language he gained from the culture in which he was raised. He never noticed how Latin sentence structures and vocabulary and the historical resonances of its phrases shaped his thinking. And when he arrived at his wondrous pronouncement, to whom was he communicating?

To be human is to be embedded inevitably in a web of communication, relationship, and interaction. Modernity revels in the freedom of the sovereign self. But modern developmental psychology has come to understand that human beings gain their sense of self-consciousness—the reality and boundaries of the self—through intimate relationships with parents and caregivers. Identity is shaped, consciously and unconsciously, by family, culture, and community. There is no such thing as a self alone. It was, after all, in her quest to marry the man she loved that Tzeitel asserted her autonomy. The discovery of relationship as the central fact of human existence belongs to the great twentieth-century Jewish thinker Martin Buber. All real life, he declared, is meeting.

> The world is twofold, in accordance with his twofold attitude.
>
> The attitude of man is twofold in accordance with the two words he can speak.
>
> The basic words are not single words but word pairs.
>
> One basic word is the word pair I-You.
>
> The other basic word is the word pair I-It.
>
> But this basic word is not changed when He or She takes the place of It.
>
> Thus the I of man is also twofold.
>
> For the I of the basic word I-You is different from that of the basic word I-It....
>
> There is no I as such but only the I of the basic word I-You and the I of the basic word I-It.[4]

Buber divides human relationships into two types. I-It relationships are functional. We know others only by what they do for us. For us, they have no interior life, no past, and no future; we experience them only on the surface, only in two dimensions. Every day we encounter the restaurant server, the supermarket checker, the bank teller, the bus driver. We don't know their stories, their aspirations, their values. They are human beings, but we perceive them only as a function. We value them for the efficiency of their function, and if we are dissatisfied, we want a replacement. Most significant, the encounter is mutual—just as the other is an It to me, I am an It to them. I am customer, passenger, client, experienced superficially and valued only for my function in their life. And I, too, am totally replaceable.

Every day is filled with I-It relationships. But sometimes we encounter a human being and something different happens. We perceive not a function but a person—a person with an interior life, a story of the past and an aspiration for a future, an individual perception of the world. This is the birth of a different relationship, what Buber called, I-You. The You is unique, irreplaceable, and precious.

> When I confront a human being as my You and speak the basic word I-You to him, then he is no thing among things nor does he consist of things. He is no longer a He or She, limited by other He's and She's, a dot in the world grid of space and time, nor a condition that can be experienced and described, a loose bundle of named qualities. Neighborless and seamless, he is You and fills the world. Not as if there were nothing but he; but everything else lives in his light.
>
> Even as a melody is not composed of tones, nor a verse of words, nor a statue of lines—one must pull and tear to turn a unity into a multiplicity—so it is with the human being to whom I say You.[5]

It is only in the I-You relationship that we discover our identity. Writes Buber, "I require a You to become; as I become I, I say You. All real living is meeting."[6] And only in the I-You relationship can we discover our uniqueness, significance, and worth. This marks every I-You relationship as a sacred moment, a religious moment. Indeed, for Buber, the I-You is the essence of religion. "In every You," writes Buber, "we address the Eternal You."[7] God is revealed in every I-You relationship.

Buber would have applauded Tzeitel's rebellion. He was profoundly anti-nomian in his understanding of religion. Rules, rites, and traditions could never capture the uniqueness and depth of relationship. They only get in the way. But he would have instructed Tzeitel to remember that the freedom won by modernity from the weight of tradition must be invested in significant relationships. The sovereign self is an illusion. The celebration of sovereignty masks a world of cold, I-It relations. The fundamental unit of human existence is not the isolated, individuated self, but the self bonded in relationship to a You. Tzeitel won her freedom and selfhood not only by breaking from tradition—that was just the first step. She finds her true, free self in loving Motel Kamzoil.

JOSEPH B. SOLOVEITCHIK: THE LONELINESS OF FAITH

When I was six years old, my brothers and I together with every child in the neighborhood lined up one afternoon in the yard of our elementary school. The school nurse gave us each a small paper cup with a sugar cube soaked in an orange liquid and instructed us to swallow it. Thus was polio eradicated from the lives of American children. Polio, the dreaded scourge, robbed the body of strength and control, bringing a lifetime of paralysis. Polio could strike anyone; even a president of the United States was its victim. In summertime, we were forbidden to swim in lakes or pools out of fear of contagion. And fear there was, until that afternoon at school.

Modern science brought the power to eradicate disease. This power is sacred. It lifts us from the vulnerable station of the brute to reshape nature—predicting its destructive whims, responding to its threats, and protecting the ones we love. That brings dignity. There is holiness in science and godliness in technology. Science is an expression of the divine commandment to rule the world and master it.

> And God created the human in God's image, in the image of God did God create him; male and female God created them. God blessed them and God said to them, "Be fertile and increase, fill the earth and master it; and rule the fish of the sea, the birds of the sky, and all the living things that creep on earth." (Genesis 1:27–28)

Hodel and Perchik sought the power to bring the chaos of nature and history under human control. That is an expression of human responsibility. Those who decry modernity and long for the simplicity of the past, for old-fashioned values and ways of life, have forgotten tuberculosis, smallpox, diphtheria, typhus, cholera, whooping cough, yellow fever, and measles. They forget how women regularly died in childbirth; how a cut finger or a broken bone brought merciless sepsis and death. There is nothing unholy in the quest for power. But that is not the entirety of human existence.

The Jewish thinker Joseph Baer Soloveitchik, scion of the greatest family of Lithuanian Talmud scholars and the revered "Rav" of American Orthodox Jewry, observed that Genesis contains two stories of human origins. The first portrays *homo faber*, creative man, who bears the image of the Creator and is commanded to gain power and control over the world. "Adam the first" seeks majesty as the ruler of the world and the dignity of a responsible life. But Adam the first describes only part of the human being. His counterpart, "Adam the second," approaches the world very differently. He asks, Why? Why am I here? What is the purpose of all this? Who do I belong to? While Adam the first is created in the image of the Creator, Adam the second is created from the dust of the earth. He is aware of his mortality, his finitude, his limitations. And where Adam the first seeks majesty and dignity, Adam the second seeks redemption—the assurance that his existence is significant despite his mortality. No accumulation of power can satisfy that quest. We gain meaning and a sense of personal significance not with the gesture of control, but to the contrary, through surrender, by giving ourselves over to something bigger. We give ourselves to others in relationship. We give ourselves over to transcendent ideals and ethics. We join our personal narratives to narratives deeper and older than our own.[8]

Like Buber, Soloveitchik perceives that modernity privileges one aspect of the human being but neglects and even derides the other. Modernity has embraced the quest of Adam the first for majesty and power but has no patience for what drives Adam the second. Thus, Soloveitchik laments, "I am lonely." In a stunningly revealing confession, Soloveitchik diagnoses the "passional experience of the contemporary man of faith."

> He looks upon himself as a stranger in a modern society, which is technically minded, self-centered, and self-loving, almost in a sickly narcissistic fashion, scorning honor upon honor, piling up victory upon victory, reaching for the distant galaxies, and seeing in the here-and-now sensible world the only manifestation of being. What can a man of faith like myself, living by a doctrine which has no technical potential, by a law which cannot be tested in the laboratory, steadfast in his loyalty to an eschatological vision whose fulfillment cannot be predicted with any degree of probability, let alone certainty, even by the most complex mathematical calculations—what can such a man say to a functional, utilitarian society which is *saeculum*-oriented and whose practical reasons of the mind have long ago supplanted the sensitive reasons of the heart?[9]

What can the man of faith say to the secular, scientific society? Power is a blessing. But the accumulation of power cannot satisfy the human need for redemption—for meaning, depth, purpose, and deep human connection. Satisfying that aspect of human being requires a different stance toward the world and a different sensibility. The accumulation of power is ultimately futile without a vision of the ends power is meant to serve. That vision does not come with power. On the contrary, the emblems of power have a way of obscuring that vision. That vision comes from a wholly different aspect of human being. Adam the first depends on Adam the second to provide that vision.

Soloveitchik would applaud Hodel and Perchik's rebellion in moving the Jewish people from passivity to activism, from being the object of history to becoming its subject. But in remaking society and rebirthing a Jewish nation, he would remind them that power alone cannot provide the most valued elements of human fulfillment. Those are won not by the conquest of nature and control of destiny but through surrender to an ideal of oneness.

ABRAHAM JOSHUA HESCHEL: RECOVERING WONDER

The tiny European gentleman, with a long mane of gray hair, a pointy gray beard, and giant black eyeglasses, would stare out, for some moments, from the rostrum of a university lecture hall, the pulpit of a great metropolitan church, or the bimah of a crowded synagogue, and then he would whisper, "Ladies and gentlemen, a great miracle just took place."

The crowd was immediately silent, arrested by this announcement, and wondering collectively what miracle could have occurred that every one of them had missed?

"A great miracle just occurred," the speaker continued, "the sun just went down."

The crowd never knew how to respond. Some smiled with amusement at this strange prophet. Some chuckled. Some sat up in curious attention.

And then the speaker proceeded to describe how a religious person sees the world. Knowledge, he explained, comes in many forms. It depends on what we wish to know. If you wish to understand the workings of the body, ask a physician. If you wish to understand love, ask a poet. Don't confuse the two. If you wish to cure heart disease, the physician has guidance to offer; the poet will lead you astray. But if you're trying to heal human loneliness, the poet can guide you; the physician can only prescribe sedatives. Religion, he declared, is a way of knowing. It is a way of answering a certain set of human questions. Our problem is that we have forgotten the questions that religion came to answer, just as we have forgotten to stop and notice the wonder of the evening's sunset.

This was how Abraham Joshua Heschel began his public lectures. Like Buber and Soloveitchik, Heschel came into modernity from the heart of traditional European Judaism. He grasped the dilemma that Chava had left behind. Freedom of mind is a great blessing. Chava, like her namesake, Mother Eve, must not be blamed for seeking knowledge, even outside the world of tradition. But once we are offered a universe of multiple truths and manifold cultures, how do we arrive at any truth? How do we make a home in the world? How do we escape the relativism that destroys all values?

Again, like Buber and Soloveitchik, Heschel understood the human condition in dualistic terms. He recognized that the dilemmas of modernity arose from its narrow definition of self. In rejecting tradition, modernity left behind the most important elements of being human. Religion today has the role of recovering what modernity left behind.

Chava, the girl with her nose pressed into a book, oblivious to the world around her, is an apt symbol of the modern self. Modernity's greatest achievements come from science. Science confronts the world dispassionately, detached. Science aims to gather objective facts about the world in order to construct conceptual models, which are useful for predicting, manipulating, and controlling the world. Science is such a powerful element of modernity that we tend to measure all knowledge by its standards.

Science, Heschel argues, is useful for knowing certain things about our world, but science cannot reach the most important human questions. Science, for example, cannot answer the scientist's own reflective questions: Why do I do science? What are the ethical uses of scientific knowledge? For questions like these, we use a different kind of knowing. This kind of knowing is not scientifically rational, nor can it be gained through dispassionate detachment. It is intensely personal. There is no safe, objective place we can stand to ask such questions. The questions arise from our own deepest life experience, and the insights we seek will shape every aspect of life.

Heschel calls this kind of knowing our "sense of the ineffable."[10] "Ineffable" means all that cannot be expressed in words. Heschel's philosophical project begins with the task describing this kind of knowing. Because the subject is beyond words, Heschel employs a peculiar vocabulary in a poetic style of writing. He points, alludes, evokes, and invites us to see our world, including its sunsets, through new eyes.

The sense of the ineffable begins in wonder.

> Wonder, or radical amazement, is the chief characteristic of the religious man's attitude toward history and nature. One attitude is alien to his spirit: taking things for granted, regarding events as a natural course of things. To find an approximate cause of a phenomenon is no answer to his ultimate wonder. He knows that there are laws that regulate the course of natural processes; he is aware of the regularity and pattern of things. However, such knowledge fails to mitigate his sense of perpetual surprise at the fact that there are facts at all.[11]

The sense of the ineffable leads us to powerful life moments that concepts cannot capture and words cannot describe. Experiences of wonder, amazement, mystery, and awe signal these extraordinary moments. These moments humble us. They diminish the sense that we have a complete understanding and control everything in our experience. They overthrow our arrogance and open us to a different kind of knowing. "Higher incomprehension," taught Heschel, is the beginning of wisdom.

> The ultimate insight is the outcome of *moments* when we are stirred beyond words, of instants of wonder, awe, praise, fear,

trembling and radical amazement; of awareness of grandeur, of perceptions we can grasp but are unable to convey, of discoveries of the unknown, of moments in which we abandon the pretense of being acquainted with the world, of *knowledge by inacquaintance*. It is at the climax of such moments that we attain the certainty that life has meaning, that time is more than evanescence, that beyond all being there is someone who cares.[12]

The peak of our sense of the ineffable is an ultimate insight, Heschel teaches. This ultimate insight is not an affirmation. It is neither an assertion of God's existence nor a validation our own significance. The ultimate insight comes as a question, demanding a response.

Religion begins with a consciousness that something is asked of us. It is in that tense, eternal asking in which the soul is caught and in which man's answer is elicited.... The more we meditate, the more clearly we realize that the question we ask is a question we are being asked; that *man's question about God is God's question of man*.[13]

Through the lens of the ineffable, the ultimate human question about God's existence is rephrased into the question God first put to Adam in Genesis: "Where are you?" (Genesis 3:9). Our search for the meaning of existence is transposed into God's search for a partner to complete the work of Creation. Our need for a sense of significance in the face of mortality is met by God's need for human participation in the divine dream of a world of oneness. The only way to answer is through action. Action, too, becomes a way of knowing.

A Jew is asked to take a *leap of action* rather than a *leap of thought*.... Through the ecstasy of deeds we learn to be certain of the hereness of God.

It is in *deeds* that man becomes aware of what his life really is.... It is in the employment of his will, not in reflection, that he meets his own self as it is, not as he should like it to be. The heart is revealed in deeds....

To meet God means to come upon an inner certainty of God's realness, an awareness of God's will. Such meeting, such presence, we experience in deeds.[14]

The only thing the Bible discloses about God, Heschel observes, is that God cares. "God in the universe is a spirit of concern for life. What is a thing to us is a concern to God."[15] But caring is more than God's. Caring is the quality human beings share with God. It is in acts of caring that the truth of our existence is revealed to us. Caring is a paradox. In performing the selfless act of caring, we come to understand the true nature and capacity of the self. Caring pushes us beyond the boundaries of the defined, narrow self, into a vision of self that includes the other. For Heschel, the act of caring is the answer to the question disclosed by our sense of the ineffable. In caring, we come to experience the meaning of our existence, the significance of our lives. In sharing the tasks of caring with God, we participate in eternity.

CHUTZPAH CHANGES EVERYTHING

Modernity celebrates the freedom of the self. But narrowing the world down to the self—the choosing self, the active self, and the knowing self—paradoxically comes to undermine this very freedom. Buber, Soloveitchik, and Heschel brought the tools of Jewish understanding to unravel this paradox. In Jewish wisdom, they located the tools to repair the modern idea of self. Buber reminds Tzeitel that only in the I-You relationship can one find the sense of personal significance that adds purpose to a life of freedom. Soloveitchik instructs Hodel that there is a realm beyond the majesty and dignity of power, and only in this realm will she locate the proper purposes to which power should be applied. And Heschel teaches Chava that real knowledge comes only from caring, from a self committed to the world.

Tevye's chutzpah, taught Buber, Soloveitchik, and Heschel, is what modernity is missing. Chutzpah, the ancient Jewish idea of the expansive self seeking oneness, the self as vessel of divine blessing, is the missing element that can save modernity from its paradoxes and its meaninglessness. At the climax of the drama of *Fiddler on the Roof,* Tevye and Golde arrive at this revelation as well.

> T: Do you love me?
> G: Do I love him?
>   For twenty-five years I've lived with him, fought
>   with him, starved with him.
>   Twenty-five years my bed is his, if that's not love
>   what is?
> T: Then you love me?
> G: I suppose I do.
> T: And I suppose I love you too.
> T & G: It doesn't change a thing but even so,
>   After twenty-five years, it's nice to know.

Actually, it changes everything. Tevye and Golde love one another not out of obligation or duty but as a choice. Tradition's ideal of oneness can be pursued in the atmosphere of modernity's freedom. That expression of chutzpah redeems modernity. And after 3,500 years, it is nice to know.

Epilogue

THE HORIZON OF HUMAN POSSIBILITY

Once upon a time in the old country, there lived a philosopher of passionate atheism who went from village to village destroying the faith of believers. No one could resist his sophistry, no faith could withstand his skepticism. Soon enough, the philosopher outgrew the challenge of overturning the belief of simpleminded villagers, and he set his sights on a higher pursuit. He announced that he would challenge the Rebbe to a disputation. Tearing down the faith of a revered spiritual master would be his life's crowning achievement.

The Rebbe's disciples came to warn him: "Beware this atheist! His arguments are shrewd, his logic is powerful, his words are seductive. Rebbe, beware this atheist!"

The Rebbe calmly dismissed their concerns. "Let him come, we'll see what he has to say."

The atheist arrived in the Rebbe's town and made his way to the Rebbe's academy. He entered into the Rebbe's chamber and found the old man sitting at a great table piled high with holy books. Just as the atheist prepared to launch into his diatribe, the Rebbe looked up into his eyes and asked him a one-word question: *"Efshar?* Is it possible?"

The atheist stopped, his attention immediately arrested. "*Efshar*? Is it possible?" he repeated to himself, "Is it possible?" His eyes filled with tears, "Is it possible?" Dropping to his knees, he began to weep and then to cry. "Yes, of course, it is possible. It is always possible. It is possible!"

The philosopher became a disciple of the Rebbe. And when anyone ever came with doubts, the philosopher would respond, "Remember, it is possible! It is always possible!"

What are the horizons of human possibility? This is the question at the heart of religion. The religious conversation does not begin with the question of God's nature or God's existence but with the question of our nature and the meaning of our existence: Do I matter? What is my purpose? What can I hope for? Only when these questions are encountered might we ask: What sort of universe would I have to imagine to support and confirm my sense of purpose, my significance? What story do I tell myself about my place in the world? What story will provide the courage to continue in the face of tragedy and disappointment, of cruelty and evil?

Judaism offers exquisite answers to these questions. Judaism places the highest significance on human being. In the language of the Bible, human beings are created in the image of God. We are God's partners in the creation of the world and responsible to protect its life. The significance of human existence is rooted in the responsibility we bear for Creation. The Rabbis of the Talmud taught:

> When God created the first man, God showed him all the trees in the Garden of Eden and said, "See how beautiful and perfect are My creations! All that I have created, I created for you. Therefore, be careful: Do not abuse or destroy My world. For if you abuse or destroy it, there is no one to repair it after you."[1]

This dual sense of exalted capacity and vast responsibility is what we have called chutzpah. Chutzpah is the very heart of Judaism. It is the source of our dignity as human beings. It provides us a sense of transcendent purpose. It gives meaning to our life struggles. It offers a way to a life that is heroic.

A COMMITMENT TO CHUTZPAH OR A MYTH OF SURRENDER

Chutzpah was born out of struggle with a very popular myth. This myth offered a severely narrow vision of human possibilities. The myth preached an ethic of moral surrender, of powerlessness and passivity. The myth was first articulated by the ancient Mesopotamians and migrated to Greek culture. From Greek culture, it found its way into the Bible itself in the resigned voice of Ecclesiastes/Kohelet.

> Utter futility! said Kohelet
>> Utter futility! All is futile!
>> What real value is there for a man in all the gains he
> makes beneath the sun?
>> One generation goes, another comes,
>> But the earth remains the same forever.
> (Ecclesiastes 1:2–4)

Wise Kohelet whispers the prudence of the realist: What is, is what is meant to be. What is, is inevitable. Nothing more is possible. Dreams and ideals are futile. Find satisfaction in private pleasures, in personal pursuits. Let the world take care of itself. Kohelet said it best:

> Go, eat your bread in gladness, and drink your wine in joy; for your action was long ago approved by God. Let your clothes always be freshly washed, and your head never lack ointment.

Enjoy happiness with a woman you love all the fleeting days of
life that have been granted to you under the sun—all your fleeting days. For that alone is what you can get out of life and out
of the means you acquire under the sun. (Ecclesiastes 9:7–9)

The ancients are gone, but the myth never died. Myths never die.
They lie dormant, waiting to find roots in new cultural soil, to
find expression in a new cultural idiom. Age after age, this myth
returns. It returns in those historical moments when the boundaries of human existence are expanded and exploded, leaving behind
an unsettled sense of existential homelessness, the soul's exile.
When the great empires of Mesopotamia supplanted the small
city-states and villages of the East, the myth was born. It returned
when the Greeks conquered and Hellenized local tribal cultures,
and again with the unrelenting Romans' march of conquest. And
it has returned again in our time, more persuasive than ever.

In our generation, we have come to recognize that our existence is no longer solely tribal or national, but global. Markets in
China and political decisions in Brazil affect the price of milk in
my corner grocery. Next door are a sushi restaurant and an Indian
café. Revolutionary technology brings the world—all its glory and
all its tragedy—into our living rooms. Environmental catastrophe
knows no borders. Chimneys in India melt icecaps in Greenland.
We have come to understand that our fate is global. And so, too,
our problems are global. Global climate change brings massive dislocation of populations, economic upheaval, and severe shortages
of food and water. International terrorism has become part of our
daily reality. We have come to dread the proliferation of nuclear,
chemical, and biological weapons of unimaginable lethality in the
hands of those who hate our civilization and its freedoms. Extreme
economic inequality erodes social cohesion, bringing political
instability and violence.

Into this confusing new milieu, the ancient myth has reemerged with virulence. To a populace confounded by global political, economic, and environmental threats, the myth confides, "Your fate is determined by forces far beyond your comprehension and control. These problems of the world are intractable. They cannot be fixed. The status quo cannot be moved. And you are certainly not responsible." It is heard in our political discourse. It is common in popular culture. It is sown deeply into our way of life. The myth counsels disengagement and resignation. It preaches the fantasy of a return to simpler times with simpler loyalties. At its worst, it devolves into crude binary thinking, reducing all problems to us against them, our people versus those people. It is cynical, hopeless, and ultimately, poisonous.

The myth renders us indifferent to the real problems that darken our future. At the same time, it erodes our humanity from within. The surrender of human possibility leaves us with a hole in the soul, a hollow emptiness within, in the place where moral purpose and human solidarity should reside. This emptiness has become a staple in our culture. We attempt to fill it with every sort of addiction—to alcohol, drugs, and gambling, to obsessive consumption, to insatiable sexual fantasy, to work. Most commonly, we seek endless distraction and entertainment. No culture in all of human history has invested more in the industry of diversion. In the Middle Ages, towns were built around a cathedral. In early modernity, a town was built around a factory. Today, the town center is the mall with its Cineplex. Once, every room in a home was protected by a religious artifact—a mezuzah on the door, a cross on the wall. Now, every room has a TV. We have no moral heroes to hold before our children. Instead, we worship entertainment celebrities. We are the culture that invented massive shopping malls and extravagant theme parks—entire cities devoted to the project of diversion—just so that we won't notice the emptiness within.

Inevitably, the myth of moral surrender leads to depression and despair. Human beings need a sense of purpose, efficacy, and significance as much as we need food, water, and oxygen. Without transcendent values, the humanity within us starves.

Today, we face a set of serious political, economic, and environmental threats. These threats become immeasurably worse when human beings come to perceive themselves as powerless to act effectively in the world and come to believe themselves immune from the responsibility. When action is displaced by distraction, and engagement by entertainment, the dangers intensify substantially. Changing the world begins by changing minds.

At the beginning of our people, Abraham was called by God: "Be a blessing.... And blessed in you shall be all the families of the earth" (Genesis 12:2–3). This is the perennial project of Jewish existence. It is the message and meaning of Jewish life. At this moment of history, we are called again. The Jewish people has a mission in the world. As the world becomes a global community, facing global dilemmas, we are called to teach chutzpah. We are called to overcome the allure of the ancient myth of moral surrender. We are called to reassert the Bible's ideal of human possibility and responsibility. It is the only way to muster the moral courage and imagination to meet the threats to our future. It is, coincidentally, the only way to revivify collective Jewish life in this moment of our history. Nostalgia for the ways and warmth of Anatevka is gone. If a new generation is to join this ancient tradition, they will join only for a message that is vital, significant, and timely. Chutzpah is that message.

As the Talmud teaches, the task is great, the stakes are exceedingly high—not only the future of the Jewish people, but also the survival of humanity. And the time is exceedingly short. We may not yet ask enough of our Judaism. But at this moment, our Judaism asks a great deal of us.

NOTES

INTRODUCTION: THE WICKED CHILD'S QUESTION

1. Pew Research Center, "A Portrait of Jewish Americans," October 1, 2013; www. pewforum.org/2013/10/01/jewish-american-beliefs-attitudes-culture-survey (accessed 07/08/2014).

2. *Pesikta de-Rav Kahana, pesikta* 12.

3. Leo Rosten, *The Joys of Yiddish* (New York: Pocket Books, 1970), pp. 92–94.

4. Jerusalem Talmud, *Taanit* 4, 69a.

5. See Talmud, *Sanhedrin* 105a.

CHAPTER ONE: HOW TO ARGUE WITH GOD AND WIN

1. James B. Pritchard, ed., *The Ancient Near East: An Anthology of Texts and Pictures,* vol. 1 (Princeton, NJ: Princeton University Press, 1973), pp. 31–33.

2. Abraham Joshua Heschel, *Man Is Not Alone* (New York: Harper and Row, 1951), p. 129.

3. *Bereishit Rabbah* 56:10, retold in Elie Wiesel, *Messengers of God* (New York: Simon and Schuster, 1985).

CHAPTER TWO: THE ROAD TO EDEN

1. *Mishnah Pesachim* 10:5.

CHAPTER THREE: JEWS GONE WILD

1. Jerusalem Talmud, *Megillah* 1.

CHAPTER FOUR: THE WORLD STANDS ON THREE PILLARS

1. *Pirkei Avot* 1:3.

2. Talmud, *Chagigah* 26b.

3. Talmud, *Baba Metzia* 59a–b.

4. Ibid., 59b.

5. Ibid.

6. Ibid.

7. Ibid.

8. Talmud, *Menachot* 29b.

9. *Avot de-Rabbi Natan* 1c.

10. *Pirkei Avot* 3:18.

11. *Tanchuma, Tazria* 5.

12. *Vayikra Rabbah* 146.

13. Talmud, *Berachot* 61b.

14. Talmud, *Berachot* 61b.

15. Talmud, *Menachot* 29b.

CHAPTER FIVE: RETURNING TO THE GARDEN

1. *Mechilta Yitro; Bereishit Rabbah.*

2. Maimonides, *Guide for the Perplexed*, trans. Shlomo Pines (Chicago: University of Chicago Press, 1963), 3:51.

3. Maimonides, *Mishneh Torah*, "Introduction," in *A Maimonides Reader*, ed. Isadore Twersky (Springfield, NJ: Behrman House, 1972), p. 35.

4. *Mishneh Torah, Yesodei Ha-Torah* 1:1.

5. Maimonides, *Guide* 1:1 (adapted from Pines trans.).

6. Ibid., 3:51 (adapted from Pines trans.).

7. Ibid., 3:31 (adapted from Pines trans.).

8. Ibid., 3:54.

9. Ibid. (Pines trans.).

10. Ibid. (adapted from Pines trans.).

11. Ibid. (adapted from Pines trans.).

12. *Bereishit Rabbah* 1:1.

13. *Mishnah Chagigah* 2:1.

14. Gershom Scholem, *Major Trends in Jewish Mysticism* (New York: Schocken Books, 1956), p. 8.

15. Adapted from Joseph Gikatilla, *Sha'are Orah, Gates of Light*, trans. Avi Weinstein (Walnut Creek, CA: Altimira Press, 1994), pp. 24–25.

16. Adapted from ibid., p. 300.

17. Zohar 2:133b–134b, in Tishby, *Wisdom of the Zohar* (London: Littman Library of Jewish Civilization, 1989), p. 1023.

18. Adapted from ibid.

19. Adapted from ibid.

20. Hayim Vital, *Sha'ar Ha-Hakdamot*, quoted in Lawrence Fine, *Physician of the Soul, Healer of the Cosmos* (Stanford, CA: Stanford University Press, 2003), p. 126.

21. Adapted from ibid.

22. *Sefer Ha-Letukim*, quoted in Scholem, *Major Trends in Jewish Mysticism*, p. 284.

23. Hayim Vital, *Sha'ar Ha-Hakdamot*, adapted from Fine, *Physician of the Soul*, p. 194.

24. Adapted from ibid., p. 250.

CHAPTER SIX: LIKE A FIDDLER ON THE ROOF

1. Robert Putman, *Bowling Alone* (New York: Touchstone Books, 2001).

2. Ahad Ha-Am, "The Jewish State and the Jewish Problem, 1897," in *The Zionist Idea*, ed. Arthur Hertzberg (New York: Atheneum Books, 1971), p. 268.

3. Ahad Ha-Am, "The People of the Book, 1894," in ibid., p. 266.

4. Martin Buber, *I and Thou*, trans. Walter Kaufmann (New York: Scribner, 1970), pp. 53–54.

5. Ibid., p. 59.

6. Adapted from Martin Buber, *I and Thou*, p. 62.

7. Ibid., p. 57.

8. Joseph B. Soloveitchik, *The Lonely Man of Faith* (originally published in *Tradition*, Summer 1965; reprinted, Northvale, NJ: Jason Aronson, 1992).

9. Ibid., p. 6.

10. Abraham Joshua Heschel, *God in Search of Man* (New York: Harper and Row, 1966), p. 20.

11. Ibid., pp. 45–46.

12. Ibid., p. 131.

13. Ibid., pp. 162, 132.

14. Ibid., p. 283.

15. Abraham Joshua Heschel, *Man Is Not Alone* (New York: Harper and Row, 1951), p. 145.

EPILOGUE: THE HORIZON OF HUMAN POSSIBILITY

1. *Kohelet Rabbah* 7:13.

SUGGESTED READING

INTRODUCTION: THE WICKED CHILD'S QUESTION

Feinstein, Edward, ed. *Jews & Judaism in the 21st Century: Human Responsibility, the Presence of God and the Future of the Covenant.* Woodstock, VT: Jewish Lights, 2007.

Schulweis, Harold. *For Those Who Can't Believe: Overcoming the Obstacles to Faith.* San Francisco: Harper, 1995.

CHAPTER ONE: HOW TO ARGUE WITH GOD AND WIN

Sarna, Nahum M. *Understanding Genesis.* New York: Schocken Books, 1970.

Wiesel, Elie. *Messengers of God: Biblical Portraits and Legends.* New York: Simon and Schuster, 1985.

CHAPTER TWO: THE ROAD TO EDEN

Greenberg, Irving. *The Jewish Way: Living the Holidays.* New York: Touchstone, 1993.

Walzer, Michael. *Exodus and Revolution.* New York: Basic Books, 1986.

CHAPTER THREE: JEWS GONE WILD

Walzer, Michael. *In God's Shadow: Politics in the Hebrew Bible.* New Haven, CT: Yale University Press, 2012.

CHAPTER FOUR: THE WORLD STANDS ON THREE PILLARS

Hartman, David. *A Living Covenant: The Innovative Spirit in Traditional Judaism.* Woodstock, VT: Jewish Lights, 1998.

CHAPTER FIVE: RETURNING TO THE GARDEN

Green, Arthur. *Ehyeh: A Kabbalah for Tomorrow.* Woodstock, VT: Jewish Lights, 2004.

Hartman, David. *Maimonides: Torah and Philosophic Quest.* Philadelphia: Jewish Publication Society, 1977.

Scholem, Gershom. *Major Trends in Jewish Mysticism.* New York: Schocken Books, 1995.

Seeskin, Kenneth. *Maimonides: A Guide for Today's Perplexed.* Springfield, NJ: Behrman House, 1996.

CHAPTER SIX: LIKE A FIDDLER ON THE ROOF

Buber, Martin. *I and Thou.* Translated by Walter Kaufman. New York: Touchstone, 1971.

Cohen, Steven M., and Arnold M. Eisen. *The Jew Within: Self, Family, and Community in America.* Bloomington: Indiana University Press, 2000.

Heschel, Abraham Joshua. *God in Search of Man: A Philosophy of Judaism.* New York: Farrar, Strauss, Giroux, 1976.

Soloveitchik, Joseph B. *The Lonely Man of Faith.* Northvale, NJ: Jason Aronson, 1992.

EPILOGUE: THE HORIZON OF HUMAN POSSIBILITY

Green, Arthur. *Radical Judaism: Rethinking God and Tradition.* New Haven: Yale University Press, 2010.

Sacks, Jonathan. *To Heal a Fractured World: The Ethics of Responsibility.* New York: Schocken Books, 2007.

Schulweis, Harold. *Conscience: The Duty to Obey and the Duty to Disobey.* Woodstock, VT: Jewish Lights, 2010.

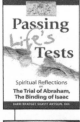

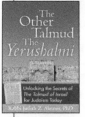

Bar / Bat Mitzvah

The Mitzvah Project Book
Making Mitzvah Part of Your Bar/Bat Mitzvah ... and Your Life
By Liz Suneby and Diane Heiman; Foreword by Rabbi Jeffrey K. Salkin; Preface by Rabbi Sharon Brous
The go-to source for Jewish young adults and their families looking to make the world a better place through good deeds—big or small.
6 x 9, 224 pp, Quality PB Original, 978-1-58023-458-0 **$16.99** *For ages 11–13*

The Bar/Bat Mitzvah Memory Book, 2nd Edition: An Album for Treasuring
the Spiritual Celebration
By Rabbi Jeffrey K. Salkin and Nina Salkin
8 x 10, 48 pp, 2-color text, Deluxe HC, ribbon marker, 978-1-58023-263-0 **$19.99**

For Kids—Putting God on Your Guest List, 2nd Edition: How to Claim the
Spiritual Meaning of Your Bar or Bat Mitzvah *By Rabbi Jeffrey K. Salkin*
6 x 9, 144 pp, Quality PB, 978-1-58023-308-8 **$15.99** *For ages 11–13*

The Jewish Prophet: Visionary Words from Moses and Miriam to Henrietta Szold
and A. J. Heschel *By Rabbi Dr. Michael J. Shire*
6½ x 8½, 128 pp, 123 full-color illus., HC, 978-1-58023-168-8 **$14.95**

Putting God on the Guest List, 3rd Edition: How to Reclaim the Spiritual
Meaning of Your Child's Bar or Bat Mitzvah *By Rabbi Jeffrey K. Salkin*
6 x 9, 224 pp, Quality PB, 978-1-58023-222-7 **$16.99**
   Teacher's Guide: 8½ x 11, 48 pp, PB, 978-1-58023-226-5 **$8.99**

Teens / Young Adults

Text Messages: A Torah Commentary for Teens
Edited by Rabbi Jeffrey K. Salkin
Shows today's teens how each Torah portion contains worlds of meaning for them, for what they are going through in their lives, and how they can shape their Jewish identity as they enter adulthood.
6 x 9, 304 pp (est), HC, 978-1-58023-507-5 **$24.99**

Hannah Senesh: Her Life and Diary, the First Complete Edition
By Hannah Senesh; Foreword by Marge Piercy; Preface by Eitan Senesh; Afterword by Roberta Grossman
6 x 9, 368 pp, b/w photos, Quality PB, 978-1-58023-342-2 **$19.99**

I Am Jewish: Personal Reflections Inspired by the Last Words of Daniel Pearl
Edited by Judea and Ruth Pearl 6 x 9, 304 pp, Deluxe PB w/ flaps, 978-1-58023-259-3 **$19.99**
Download a free copy of the *I Am Jewish Teacher's Guide* at www.jewishlights.com.

The JGirl's Guide: The Young Jewish Woman's Handbook for Coming of Age
By Penina Adelman, Ali Feldman and Shulamit Reinharz
6 x 9, 240 pp, Quality PB, 978-1-58023-215-9 **$16.99** *For ages 11 & up*
   Teacher's & Parent's Guide: 8½ x 11, 56 pp, PB, 978-1-58023-225-8 **$8.99**

The JGuy's Guide: The GPS for Jewish Teen Guys
By Rabbi Joseph B. Meszler, Dr. Shulamit Reinharz, Liz Suneby and Diane Heiman
6 x 9, 208 pp, Quality PB Original, 978-1-58023-721-5 **$16.99**
   Teacher's Guide: 8½ x 11, 30pp, PB, 978-1-58023-773-4 **$8.99**

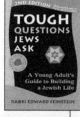

Tough Questions Jews Ask, 2nd Edition: A Young Adult's Guide to Building a
Jewish Life *By Rabbi Edward Feinstein*
6 x 9, 160 pp, Quality PB, 978-1-58023-454-2 **$16.99** *For ages 11 & up*
   Teacher's Guide: 8½ x 11, 72 pp, PB, 978-1-58023-187-9 **$8.95**

Pre-Teens

Be Like God: God's To-Do List for Kids
By Dr. Ron Wolfson
Encourages kids ages eight through twelve to use their God-given superpowers to find the many ways they can make a difference in the lives of others and find meaning and purpose for their own.
7 x 9, 144 pp, Quality PB, 978-1-58023-510-5 **$15.99** *For ages 8–12*

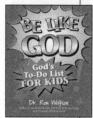

The Book of Miracles: A Young Person's Guide to Jewish Spiritual Awareness
By Lawrence Kushner, with all-new illustrations by the author.
6 x 9, 96 pp, 2-color illus., HC, 978-1-879045-78-1 **$16.95** *For ages 9–13*

Children's Books

Around the World in One Shabbat
Jewish People Celebrate the Sabbath Together
By Durga Yael Bernhard

Takes your child on a colorful adventure to share the many ways Jewish people celebrate Shabbat around the world.

11 x 8½, 32 pp, Full-color illus., HC, 978-1-58023-433-7 **$18.99** *For ages 3–6*

It's a ... It's a ... It's a Mitzvah
By Liz Suneby and Diane Heiman; Full-color Illus. by Laurel Molk

Join Mitzvah Meerkat and friends as they introduce children to the everyday kindnesses that mark the beginning of a Jewish journey and a lifetime commitment to *tikkun olam* (repairing the world). 9 x 12, 32 pp, Full-color illus., HC, 978-1-58023-509-9 **$18.99** *For ages 3–6*

What You Will See Inside a Synagogue
By Rabbi Lawrence A. Hoffman, PhD, and Dr. Ron Wolfson; Full-color photos by Bill Aron

A colorful, fun-to-read introduction that explains the ways and whys of Jewish worship and religious life. 8½ x 10½, 32 pp, Full-color photos, Quality PB, 978-1-59473-256-0 **$8.99** *For ages 6 & up*
(A book from SkyLight Paths, Jewish Lights' sister imprint)

Because Nothing Looks Like God
By Lawrence Kushner and Karen Kushner

Real-life examples of happiness and sadness—from goodnight stories, to the hope and fear felt the first time at bat, to the closing moments of someone's life—invite parents and children to explore, together, the questions we all have about God, no matter what our age. 11 x 8¾, 32 pp, Full-color illus., HC, 978-1-58023-092-6 **$18.99** *For ages 4 & up*

The Book of Miracles: A Young Person's Guide to Jewish Spiritual Awareness
Written and illus. by Lawrence Kushner

Easy-to-read, imaginatively illustrated book encourages kids' awareness of their own spirituality. Revealing the essence of Judaism in a language they can understand and enjoy. 6 x 9, 96 pp, 2-color illus., HC, 978-1-879045-78-1 **$16.95** *For ages 9–13*

In God's Hands *By Lawrence Kushner and Gary Schmidt*

Brings new life to a traditional Jewish folktale, reminding parents and kids of all faiths and all backgrounds that each of us has the power to make the world a better place—working ordinary miracles with our everyday deeds. 9 x 12, 32 pp, Full-color illus., HC, 978-1-58023-224-1 **$16.99** *For ages 5 & up*

In Our Image: God's First Creatures
By Nancy Sohn Swartz

A playful new twist to the Genesis story, God asks all of nature to offer gifts to humankind—with a promise that the humans would care for creation in return. 9 x 12, 32 pp, Full-color illus., HC, 978-1-879045-99-6 **$16.95** *For ages 4 & up*
Animated app available on Apple App Store and The Google Play Marketplace **$9.99**

The Jewish Family Fun Book, 2nd Ed.
Holiday Projects, Everyday Activities, and Travel Ideas with Jewish Themes
By Danielle Dardashti and Roni Sarig

The complete sourcebook for families wanting to put a new spin on activities for Jewish holidays, holy days and the everyday. It offers dozens of easy-to-do activities that bring Jewish tradition to life for kids of all ages.

6 x 9, 304 pp, w/ 70+ b/w illus., Quality PB, 978-1-58023-333-0 **$18.99**

What Makes Someone a Jew? *By Lauren Seidman*

Reflects the changing face of American Judaism. Helps preschoolers and young readers (ages 3–6) understand that you don't have to look a certain way to be Jewish.

10 x 8½, 32 pp, Full-color photos, Quality PB, 978-1-58023-321-7 **$8.99** *For ages 3–6*

When a Grandparent Dies: A Kid's Own Remembering Workbook for
Dealing with Shiva and the Year Beyond *By Nechama Liss-Levinson*
8 x 10, 48 pp, 2-color text, HC, 978-1-879045-44-6 **$15.95** *For ages 7–13*

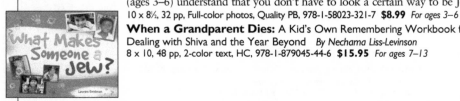

Meditation

The Magic of Hebrew Chant: Healing the Spirit, Transforming the Mind, Deepening Love
By Rabbi Shefa Gold; Foreword by Sylvia Boorstein
Introduces this transformative spiritual practice as a way to unlock the power of sacred texts and make prayer and meditation the delight of your life. Includes musical notations. 6 x 9, 352 pp, Quality PB, 978-1-58023-671-3 **$24.99**

The Magic of Hebrew Chant Companion—The Big Book of Musical Notations and Incantations
8½ x 11, 154 pp, PB, 978-1-58023-722-2 **$19.99**

Jewish Meditation Practices for Everyday Life: Awakening Your Heart, Connecting with God
By Rabbi Jeff Roth
Offers a fresh take on meditation that draws on life experience and living life with greater clarity as opposed to the traditional method of rigorous study.
6 x 9, 224 pp, Quality PB, 978-1-58023-397-2 **$18.99**

Discovering Jewish Meditation, 2nd Edition
Instruction & Guidance for Learning an Ancient Spiritual Practice
By Nan Fink Gefen, PhD 6 x 9, 208 pp, Quality PB, 978-1-58023-462-7 **$16.99**

The Handbook of Jewish Meditation Practices
A Guide for Enriching the Sabbath and Other Days of Your Life
By Rabbi David A. Cooper 6 x 9, 208 pp, Quality PB, 978-1-58023-102-2 **$16.95**

Meditation from the Heart of Judaism
Today's Teachers Share Their Practices, Techniques, and Faith
Edited by Avram Davis 6 x 9, 256 pp, Quality PB, 978-1-58023-049-0 **$18.99**

Ritual / Sacred Practices

God in Your Body: Kabbalah, Mindfulness and Embodied Spiritual Practice
By Jay Michaelson
The first comprehensive treatment of the body in Jewish spiritual practice and an essential guide to the sacred. 6 x 9, 272 pp, Quality PB, 978-1-58023-304-0 **$18.99**

The Book of Jewish Sacred Practices: CLAL's Guide to Everyday & Holiday Rituals & Blessings *Edited by Rabbi Irwin Kula and Vanessa L. Ochs, PhD*
6 x 9, 368 pp, Quality PB, 978-1-58023-152-7 **$18.95**

The Jewish Dream Book: The Key to Opening the Inner Meaning of Your Dreams
By Vanessa L. Ochs, PhD, with Elizabeth Ochs; Illus. by Kristina Swarner
8 x 8, 128 pp, Full-color illus., Deluxe PB w/ flaps, 978-1-58023-132-9 **$16.95**

Jewish Ritual: A Brief Introduction for Christians
By Rabbi Kerry M. Olitzky and Rabbi Daniel Judson
5½ x 8½, 144 pp, Quality PB, 978-1-58023-210-4 **$14.99**

The Rituals & Practices of a Jewish Life: A Handbook for Personal Spiritual Renewal *Edited by Rabbi Kerry M. Olitzky and Rabbi Daniel Judson*
6 x 9, 272 pp, Illus., Quality PB, 978-1-58023-169-5 **$18.95**

The Sacred Art of Lovingkindness: Preparing to Practice
By Rabbi Rami Shapiro 5½ x 8½, 176 pp, Quality PB, 978-1-59473-151-8 **$16.99***

Mystery & Detective Fiction

Criminal Kabbalah: An Intriguing Anthology of Jewish Mystery & Detective Fiction *Edited by Lawrence W. Raphael; Foreword by Laurie R. King*
All-new stories from twelve of today's masters of mystery and detective fiction—sure to delight mystery buffs of all faith traditions.
6 x 9, 256 pp, Quality PB, 978-1-58023-109-1 **$16.95**

Mystery Midrash: An Anthology of Jewish Mystery & Detective Fiction
Edited by Lawrence W. Raphael; Preface by Joel Siegel
6 x 9, 304 pp, Quality PB, 978-1-58023-055-1 **$16.95**

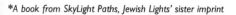

*A book from SkyLight Paths, Jewish Lights' sister imprint

Theology / Philosophy / The Way Into... Series

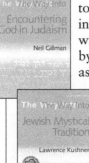

The Way Into... series offers an accessible and highly usable "guided tour" of the Jewish faith, people, history and beliefs—in total, an introduction to Judaism that will enable you to understand and interact with the sacred texts of the Jewish tradition. Each volume is written by a leading contemporary scholar and teacher, and explores one key aspect of Judaism. The Way Into... series enables all readers to achieve a real sense of Jewish cultural literacy through guided study.

The Way Into Encountering God in Judaism
By Rabbi Neil Gillman, PhD
For everyone who wants to understand how Jews have encountered God throughout history and today.
6 x 9, 240 pp, Quality PB, 978-1-58023-199-2 **$18.99**; HC, 978-1-58023-025-4 **$21.95**
Also Available: **The Jewish Approach to God:** A Brief Introduction for Christians
By Rabbi Neil Gillman, PhD
5½ x 8½, 192 pp, Quality PB, 978-1-58023-190-9 **$16.95**

The Way Into Jewish Mystical Tradition
By Rabbi Lawrence Kushner
Allows readers to interact directly with the sacred mystical texts of the Jewish tradition. An accessible introduction to the concepts of Jewish mysticism, their religious and spiritual significance, and how they relate to life today.
6 x 9, 224 pp, Quality PB, 978-1-58023-200-5 **$18.99**

The Way Into Jewish Prayer
By Rabbi Lawrence A. Hoffman, PhD
Opens the door to 3,000 years of Jewish prayer, making anyone feel at home in the Jewish way of communicating with God.
6 x 9, 208 pp, Quality PB, 978-1-58023-201-2 **$18.99**

The Way Into Jewish Prayer Teacher's Guide
By Rabbi Jennifer Ossakow Goldsmith
8½ x 11, 42 pp, PB, 978-1-58023-345-3 **$8.99**
Download a free copy at www.jewishlights.com.

The Way Into Judaism and the Environment
By Jeremy Benstein, PhD
Explores the ways in which Judaism contributes to contemporary social-environmental issues, the extent to which Judaism is part of the problem and how it can be part of the solution.
6 x 9, 288 pp, Quality PB, 978-1-58023-368-2 **$18.99**; HC, 978-1-58023-268-5 **$24.99**

The Way Into *Tikkun Olam* (Repairing the World)
By Rabbi Elliot N. Dorff, PhD
An accessible introduction to the Jewish concept of the individual's responsibility to care for others and repair the world.
6 x 9, 304 pp, Quality PB, 978-1-58023-328-6 **$18.99**

The Way Into Torah
By Rabbi Norman J. Cohen, PhD
Helps guide you in the exploration of the origins and development of Torah, explains why it should be studied and how to do it.
6 x 9, 176 pp, Quality PB, 978-1-58023-198-5 **$16.99**

The Way Into the Varieties of Jewishness
By Sylvia Barack Fishman, PhD
Explores the religious and historical understanding of what it has meant to be Jewish from ancient times to the present controversy over "Who is a Jew?"
6 x 9, 288 pp, Quality PB, 978-1-58023-367-5 **$18.99**; HC, 978-1-58023-030-8 **$24.99**

Theology / Philosophy

Believing and Its Tensions: A Personal Conversation about God, Torah, Suffering and Death in Jewish Thought
By Rabbi Neil Gillman, PhD
Explores the changing nature of belief and the complexities of reconciling the intellectual, emotional and moral questions of Gillman's own searching mind and soul.
5½ x 8½, 144 pp, HC, 978-1-58023-669-0 **$19.99**

God of Becoming and Relationship: The Dynamic Nature of Process Theology   *By Rabbi Bradley Shavit Artson, DHL*
Explains how Process Theology breaks us free from the strictures of ancient Greek and medieval European philosophy, allowing us to see all creation as related patterns of energy through which we connect to everything.
6 x 9, 208 pp, HC, 978-1-58023-713-0 **$24.99**

The Other Talmud—The *Yerushalmi*: Unlocking the Secrets of *The Talmud of Israel* for Judaism Today   *By Rabbi Judith Z. Abrams, PhD*
A fascinating—and stimulating—look at "the other Talmud" and the possibilities for Jewish life reflected there.   6 x 9, 256 pp, HC, 978-1-58023-463-4 **$24.99**

The Way of Man: According to Hasidic Teaching
By Martin Buber; New Translation and Introduction by Rabbi Bernard H. Mehlman and Dr. Gabriel E. Padawer; Foreword by Paul Mendes-Flohr
An accessible and engaging new translation of Buber's classic work—*available as an eBook only.*   eBook, 978-1-58023-601-0 Digital List Price **$14.99**

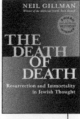

The Death of Death: Resurrection and Immortality in Jewish Thought
By Rabbi Neil Gillman, PhD 6 x 9, 336 pp, Quality PB, 978-1-58023-081-0 **$19.99**

Doing Jewish Theology: God, Torah & Israel in Modern Judaism *By Rabbi Neil Gillman, PhD*
6 x 9, 304 pp, Quality PB, 978-1-58023-439-9 **$18.99**; HC, 978-1-58023-322-4 **$24.99**

From Defender to Critic: The Search for a New Jewish Self
By Dr. David Hartman 6 x 9, 336 pp, HC, 978-1-58023-515-0 **$35.00**

The God Who Hates Lies: Confronting & Rethinking Jewish Tradition
By Dr. David Hartman with Charlie Buckholtz 6 x 9, 208 pp, Quality PB, 978-1-58023-790-1 **$19.99**

A Heart of Many Rooms: Celebrating the Many Voices within Judaism
By Dr. David Hartman 6 x 9, 352 pp, Quality PB, 978-1-58023-156-5 **$19.95**

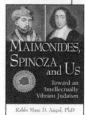

Jewish Theology in Our Time: A New Generation Explores the Foundations and Future of Jewish Belief   *Edited by Rabbi Elliot J. Cosgrove, PhD; Foreword by Rabbi David J. Wolpe; Preface by Rabbi Carole B. Balin, PhD* 6 x 9, 240 pp, Quality PB, 978-1-58023-630-0 **$19.99**; HC, 978-1-58023-413-9 **$24.99**

Maimonides—Essential Teachings on Jewish Faith & Ethics: The Book of Knowledge & the Thirteen Principles of Faith—Annotated & Explained
Translation and Annotation by Rabbi Marc D. Angel, PhD
5½ x 8½, 224 pp, Quality PB Original, 978-1-59473-311-6 **$18.99***

Maimonides, Spinoza and Us: Toward an Intellectually Vibrant Judaism
By Rabbi Marc D. Angel, PhD 6 x 9, 224 pp, HC, 978-1-58023-411-5 **$24.99**

Our Religious Brains: What Cognitive Science Reveals about Belief, Morality, Community and Our Relationship with God
By Rabbi Ralph D. Mecklenburger; Foreword by Dr. Howard Kelfer; Preface by Dr. Neil Gillman
6 x 9, 224 pp, HC, 978-1-58023-508-2 **$24.99**

Your Word Is Fire: The Hasidic Masters on Contemplative Prayer
Edited and translated by Rabbi Arthur Green, PhD, and Barry W. Holtz
6 x 9, 160 pp, Quality PB, 978-1-879045-25-5 **$16.99**

I Am Jewish
Personal Reflections Inspired by the Last Words of Daniel Pearl
Almost 150 Jews—both famous and not—from all walks of life, from all around the world, write about many aspects of their Judaism.
   Edited by Judea and Ruth Pearl   6 x 9, 304 pp, Deluxe PB w/ flaps, 978-1-58023-259-3 **$19.99**
Download a free copy of the *I Am Jewish Teacher's Guide* at www.jewishlights.com.

**A book from SkyLight Paths, Jewish Lights' sister imprint*

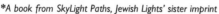

Life Cycle

Marriage / Parenting / Family / Aging

The New Jewish Baby Album: Creating and Celebrating the Beginning of a Spiritual Life—A Jewish Lights Companion
By the Editors at Jewish Lights; Foreword by Anita Diamant; Preface by Rabbi Sandy Eisenberg Sasso
A spiritual keepsake that will be treasured for generations. More than just a memory book, *shows you how—and why it's important*—to create a Jewish home and a Jewish life. 8 x 10, 64 pp, Deluxe Padded HC, Full-color illus., 978-1-58023-138-1 **$19.95**

The Jewish Pregnancy Book: A Resource for the Soul, Body & Mind during Pregnancy, Birth & the First Three Months *By Sandy Falk, MD, and Rabbi Daniel Judson, with Steven A. Rapp* Medical information, prayers and rituals for each stage of pregnancy. 7 x 10, 208 pp, b/w photos, Quality PB, 978-1-58023-178-7 **$16.95**

Celebrating Your New Jewish Daughter: Creating Jewish Ways to Welcome Baby Girls into the Covenant—New and Traditional Ceremonies *By Debra Nussbaum Cohen; Foreword by Rabbi Sandy Eisenberg Sasso* 6 x 9, 272 pp, Quality PB, 978-1-58023-090-2 **$18.95**

The New Jewish Baby Book, 2nd Edition: Names, Ceremonies & Customs—A Guide for Today's Families *By Anita Diamant* 6 x 9, 320 pp, Quality PB, 978-1-58023-251-7 **$19.99**

Parenting Jewish Teens: A Guide for the Perplexed
By Joanne Doades Explores the questions and issues that shape the world in which today's Jewish teenagers live and offers constructive advice to parents.
6 x 9, 176 pp, Quality PB, 978-1-58023-305-7 **$16.99**

Judaism for Two: A Spiritual Guide for Strengthening and Celebrating Your Loving Relationship *By Rabbi Nancy Fuchs-Kreimer, PhD, and Rabbi Nancy H. Wiener, DMin; Foreword by Rabbi Elliot N. Dorff, PhD*
Addresses the ways Jewish teachings can enhance and strengthen committed relationships. 6 x 9, 224 pp, Quality PB, 978-1-58023-254-8 **$16.99**

The Creative Jewish Wedding Book, 2nd Edition: A Hands-On Guide to New & Old Traditions, Ceremonies & Celebrations *By Gabrielle Kaplan-Mayer* 9 x 9, 288 pp, b/w photos, Quality PB, 978-1-58023-398-9 **$19.99**

Divorce Is a Mitzvah: A Practical Guide to Finding Wholeness and Holiness When Your Marriage Dies *By Rabbi Perry Netter; Afterword by Rabbi Laura Geller* 6 x 9, 224 pp, Quality PB, 978-1-58023-172-5 **$18.99**

Embracing the Covenant: Converts to Judaism Talk About Why & How *By Rabbi Allan Berkowitz and Patti Moskovitz* 6 x 9, 192 pp, Quality PB, 978-1-879045-50-7 **$16.95**

A Heart of Wisdom: Making the Jewish Journey from Midlife through the Elder Years *Edited by Susan Berrin; Foreword by Rabbi Harold Kushner* 6 x 9, 384 pp, Quality PB, 978-1-58023-051-3 **$18.95**

Introducing My Faith and My Community: The Jewish Outreach Institute Guide for the Christian in a Jewish Interfaith Relationship
By Rabbi Kerry M. Olitzky 6 x 9, 176 pp, Quality PB, 978-1-58023-192-3 **$16.99**

Jewish Visions for Aging: A Professional Guide for Fostering Wholeness *By Rabbi Dale A. Friedman, MSW, MAJCS, BCC; Foreword by Thomas R. Cole, PhD; Preface by Dr. Eugene B. Borowitz*
6 x 9, 272 pp, HC, 978-1-58023-348-4 **$24.99**

Making a Successful Jewish Interfaith Marriage: The Jewish Outreach Institute Guide to Opportunities, Challenges and Resources *By Rabbi Kerry M. Olitzky with Joan Peterson Littman* 6 x 9, 176 pp, Quality PB, 978-1-58023-170-1 **$16.95**

A Man's Responsibility: A Jewish Guide to Being a Son, a Partner in Marriage, a Father and a Community Leader *By Rabbi Joseph B. Meszler*
6 x 9, 192 pp, Quality PB, 978-1-58023-435-1 **$16.99**

So That Your Values Live On: Ethical Wills and How to Prepare Them *Edited by Rabbi Jack Riemer and Rabbi Nathaniel Stampfer*
6 x 9, 272 pp, Quality PB, 978-1-879045-34-7 **$18.99**

Holidays / Holy Days

Prayers of Awe Series

An exciting new series that examines the High Holy Day liturgy to enrich the praying experience of everyone—whether experienced worshipers or guests who encounter Jewish prayer for the very first time.

May God Remember: Memory and Memorializing in Judaism—*Yizkor*
Edited by Rabbi Lawrence A. Hoffman, PhD
Examines the history and ideas behind *Yizkor*, the Jewish memorial service, and this fascinating chapter in Jewish piety.
6 x 9, 304 pp, HC, 978-1-58023-689-8 **$24.99**

We Have Sinned—Sin and Confession in Judaism: *Ashamnu* and *Al Chet*
Edited by Rabbi Lawrence A. Hoffman, PhD 6 x 9, 304 pp, HC, 978-1-58023-612-6 **$24.99**

Who by Fire, Who by Water—*Un'taneh Tokef*
Edited by Rabbi Lawrence A. Hoffman, PhD
6 x 9, 272 pp, Quality PB, 978-1-58023-672-0 **$19.99**; HC, 978-1-58023-424-5 **$24.99**

All These Vows—*Kol Nidre*
Edited by Rabbi Lawrence A. Hoffman, PhD 6 x 9, 288 pp, HC, 978-1-58023-430-6 **$24.99**

Rosh Hashanah Readings: Inspiration, Information and Contemplation
Yom Kippur Readings: Inspiration, Information and Contemplation
Edited by Rabbi Dov Peretz Elkins; Section Introductions from Arthur Green's These Are the Words
Rosh Hashanah: 6 x 9, 400 pp, Quality PB, 978-1-58023-437-5 **$19.99**
Yom Kippur: 6 x 9, 368 pp, Quality PB, 978-1-58023-438-2 **$19.99**; HC, 978-1-58023-271-5 **$24.99**

Reclaiming Judaism as a Spiritual Practice: Holy Days and Shabbat
By Rabbi Goldie Milgram 7 x 9, 272 pp, Quality PB, 978-1-58023-205-0 **$19.99**

The Sabbath Soul: Mystical Reflections on the Transformative Power of Holy Time
Selection, Translation and Commentary by Eitan Fishbane, PhD
6 x 9, 208 pp, Quality PB, 978-1-58023-459-7 **$18.99**

Shabbat, 2nd Edition: The Family Guide to Preparing for and Celebrating the Sabbath
By Dr. Ron Wolfson 7 x 9, 320 pp, Illus., Quality PB, 978-1-58023-164-0 **$21.99**

Hanukkah, 2nd Edition: The Family Guide to Spiritual Celebration
By Dr. Ron Wolfson 7 x 9, 240 pp, Illus., Quality PB, 978-1-58023-122-0 **$18.95**

Passover

My People's Passover Haggadah
Traditional Texts, Modern Commentaries
Edited by Rabbi Lawrence A. Hoffman, PhD, and David Arnow, PhD
A diverse and exciting collection of commentaries on the traditional Passover Haggadah—in two volumes!
Vol. 1: 7 x 10, 304 pp, HC, 978-1-58023-354-5 **$24.99**
Vol. 2: 7 x 10, 320 pp, HC, 978-1-58023-346-0 **$24.99**

Creating Lively Passover Seders, 2nd Edition: A Sourcebook of Engaging Tales, Texts & Activities *By David Arnow, PhD* 7 x 9, 464 pp, Quality PB, 978-1-58023-444-3 **$24.99**

Freedom Journeys: The Tale of Exodus and Wilderness across Millennia
By Rabbi Arthur O. Waskow and Rabbi Phyllis O. Berman
6 x 9, 288 pp, HC, 978-1-58023-445-0 **$24.99**

Leading the Passover Journey: The Seder's Meaning Revealed, the Haggadah's
Story Retold *By Rabbi Nathan Laufer*
6 x 9, 224 pp, Quality PB, 978-1-58023-399-6 **$18.99**

Passover, 2nd Edition: The Family Guide to Spiritual Celebration
By Dr. Ron Wolfson with Joel Lurie Grishaver 7 x 9, 416 pp, Quality PB, 978-1-58023-174-9 **$19.95**

The Women's Passover Companion: Women's Reflections on the Festival of Freedom
Edited by Rabbi Sharon Cohen Anisfeld, Tara Mohr and Catherine Spector; Foreword by Paula E. Hyman
6 x 9, 352 pp, Quality PB, 978-1-58023-231-9 **$19.99**; HC, 978-1-58023-128-2 **$24.95**

The Women's Seder Sourcebook: Rituals & Readings for Use at the Passover Seder
Edited by Rabbi Sharon Cohen Anisfeld, Tara Mohr and Catherine Spector
6 x 9, 384 pp, Quality PB, 978-1-58023-232-6 **$19.99**

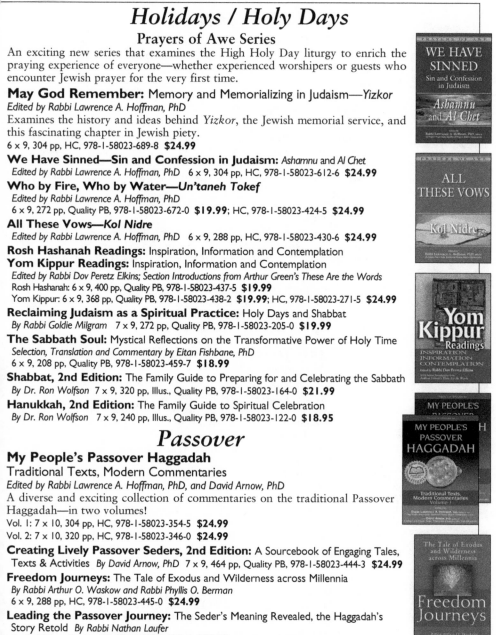

Social Justice

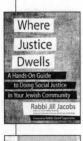

Where Justice Dwells
A Hands-On Guide to Doing Social Justice in Your Jewish Community
By Rabbi Jill Jacobs; Foreword by Rabbi David Saperstein
Provides ways to envision and act on your own ideals of social justice.
7 x 9, 288 pp, Quality PB Original, 978-1-58023-453-5 **$24.99**

There Shall Be No Needy
Pursuing Social Justice through Jewish Law and Tradition
By Rabbi Jill Jacobs; Foreword by Rabbi Elliot N. Dorff, PhD; Preface by Simon Greer
Confronts the most pressing issues of twenty-first-century America from a deeply Jewish perspective. 6 x 9, 288 pp, Quality PB, 978-1-58023-425-2 **$16.99**

There Shall Be No Needy Teacher's Guide 8½ x 11, 56 pp, PB, 978-1-58023-429-0 **$8.99**

Conscience
The Duty to Obey and the Duty to Disobey
By Rabbi Harold M. Schulweis
Examines the idea of conscience and the role conscience plays in our relationships to government, law, ethics, religion, human nature, God—and to each other.
6 x 9, 160 pp, Quality PB, 978-1-58023-419-1 **$16.99**; HC, 978-1-58023-375-0 **$19.99**

Judaism and Justice
The Jewish Passion to Repair the World
By Rabbi Sidney Schwarz; Foreword by Ruth Messinger
Explores the relationship between Judaism, social justice and the Jewish identity of American Jews. 6 x 9, 352 pp, Quality PB, 978-1-58023-353-8 **$19.99**

Spirituality / Women's Interest

New Jewish Feminism
Probing the Past, Forging the Future
Edited by Rabbi Elyse Goldstein; Foreword by Anita Diamant
Looks at the growth and accomplishments of Jewish feminism and what they mean for Jewish women today and tomorrow.
6 x 9, 480 pp, HC, 978-1-58023-359-0 **$24.99**

The Divine Feminine in Biblical Wisdom Literature
Selections Annotated & Explained
Translation & Annotation by Rabbi Rami Shapiro
5½ x 8½, 240 pp, Quality PB, 978-1-59473-109-9 **$16.99***

The Quotable Jewish Woman
Wisdom, Inspiration & Humor from the Mind & Heart
Edited by Elaine Bernstein Partnow
6 x 9, 496 pp, Quality PB, 978-1-58023-236-4 **$19.99**

The Women's Haftarah Commentary
New Insights from Women Rabbis on the 54 Weekly Haftarah Portions, the 5 Megillot & Special Shabbatot
Edited by Rabbi Elyse Goldstein
Illuminates the historical significance of female portrayals in the Haftarah and the Five Megillot. 6 x 9, 560 pp, Quality PB, 978-1-58023-371-2 **$19.99**

The Women's Torah Commentary
New Insights from Women Rabbis on the 54 Weekly Torah Portions
Edited by Rabbi Elyse Goldstein
Over fifty women rabbis offer inspiring insights on the Torah, in a week-by-week format.
6 x 9, 496 pp, Quality PB, 978-1-58023-370-5 **$19.99**; HC, 978-1-58023-076-6 **$34.95**

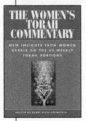

See Passover for *The Women's Passover Companion: Women's Reflections on the Festival of Freedom* and *The Women's Seder Sourcebook: Rituals & Readings for Use at the Passover Seder.*

*A book from SkyLight Paths, Jewish Lights' sister imprint

Spirituality / Prayer

Davening: A Guide to Meaningful Jewish Prayer
By Rabbi Zalman Schachter-Shalomi with Joel Segel; Foreword by Rabbi Lawrence Kushner
A fresh approach to prayer for all who wish to appreciate the power of prayer's poetry, song and ritual, and to join the age-old conversation that Jews have had with God. 6 x 9, 240 pp, Quality PB, 978-1-58023-627-0 **$18.99**

Jewish Men Pray: Words of Yearning, Praise, Petition, Gratitude and Wonder from Traditional and Contemporary Sources
Edited by Rabbi Kerry M. Olitzky and Stuart M. Matlins; Foreword by Rabbi Bradley Shavit Artson, DHL
A celebration of Jewish men's voices in prayer—to strengthen, heal, comfort, and inspire—from the ancient world up to our own day.
5 x 7¼, 400 pp, HC, 978-1-58023-628-7 **$19.99**

Making Prayer Real: Leading Jewish Spiritual Voices on Why Prayer Is Difficult and What to Do about It *By Rabbi Mike Comins* 6 x 9, 320 pp, Quality PB, 978-1-58023-417-7 **$18.99**

Witnesses to the One: The Spiritual History of the *Sh'ma*
By Rabbi Joseph B. Meszler; Foreword by Rabbi Elyse Goldstein
6 x 9, 176 pp, Quality PB, 978-1-58023-400-9 **$16.99**; HC, 978-1-58023-309-5 **$19.99**

My People's Prayer Book Series: Traditional Prayers, Modern Commentaries *Edited by Rabbi Lawrence A. Hoffman, PhD*

Provides diverse and exciting commentary to the traditional liturgy. Will help you find new wisdom in Jewish prayer, and bring liturgy into your life. Each book includes Hebrew text, modern translations and commentaries from all perspectives of the Jewish world.

Vol. 1—The *Sh'ma* and Its Blessings
 7 x 10, 168 pp, HC, 978-1-879045-79-8 **$29.99**
Vol. 2—The *Amidah* 7 x 10, 240 pp, HC, 978-1-879045-80-4 **$29.99**
Vol. 3—*P'sukei D'zimrah* (Morning Psalms)
 7 x 10, 240 pp, HC, 978-1-879045-81-1 **$29.99**
Vol. 4—*Seder K'riat Hatorah* (The Torah Service)
 7 x 10, 264 pp, HC, 978-1-879045-82-8 **$29.99**
Vol. 5—*Birkhot Hashachar* (Morning Blessings)
 7 x 10, 240 pp, HC, 978-1-879045-83-5 **$24.95**
Vol. 6—*Tachanun* and Concluding Prayers
 7 x 10, 240 pp, HC, 978-1-879045-84-2 **$24.95**
Vol. 7—Shabbat at Home 7 x 10, 240 pp, HC, 978-1-879045-85-9 **$29.99**
Vol. 8—*Kabbalat Shabbat* (Welcoming Shabbat in the Synagogue)
 7 x 10, 240 pp, HC, 978-1-58023-121-3 **$24.99**
Vol. 9—Welcoming the Night: *Minchah* and *Ma'ariv* (Afternoon and
 Evening Prayer) 7 x 10, 272 pp, HC, 978-1-58023-262-3 **$24.99**
Vol. 10—Shabbat Morning: *Shacharit* and *Musaf* (Morning and
 Additional Services) 7 x 10, 240 pp, HC, 978-1-58023-240-1 **$29.99**

Spirituality / Lawrence Kushner

I'm God; You're Not: Observations on Organized Religion & Other Disguises of the Ego
6 x 9, 256 pp, Quality PB, 978-1-58023-513-6 **$18.99**; HC, 978-1-58023-441-2 **$21.99**

The Book of Letters: A Mystical Hebrew Alphabet
Popular HC Edition, 6 x 9, 80 pp, 2-color text, 978-1-879045-00-2 **$24.95**
 Collector's Limited Edition, 9 x 12, 80 pp, gold-foil-embossed pages, w/ limited-edition silkscreened print, 978-1-879045-04-0 **$349.00**

The Book of Miracles: A Young Person's Guide to Jewish Spiritual Awareness
6 x 9, 96 pp, 2-color illus., HC, 978-1-879045-78-1 **$16.95** *For ages 9–13*

God Was in This Place & I, i Did Not Know: Finding Self, Spirituality and
 Ultimate Meaning 6 x 9, 192 pp, Quality PB, 978-1-879045-33-0 **$16.95**

Honey from the Rock: An Introduction to Jewish Mysticism
6 x 9, 176 pp, Quality PB, 978-1-58023-073-5 **$18.99**

Invisible Lines of Connection: Sacred Stories of the Ordinary
5½ x 8½, 160 pp, Quality PB, 978-1-879045-98-9 **$16.99**

The Way Into Jewish Mystical Tradition
6 x 9, 224 pp, Quality PB, 978-1-58023-200-5 **$18.99**; HC, 978-1-58023-029-2 **$21.95**

Inspiration

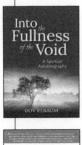

Into the Fullness of the Void: A Spiritual Autobiography *By Dov Elbaum*
The spiritual autobiography of one of Israel's leading cultural figures that provides insights and guidance for all of us. 6 x 9, 304 pp, Quality PB Original, 978-1-58023-715-4 **$18.99**

Saying No and Letting Go: Jewish Wisdom on Making Room for What Matters Most *By Rabbi Edwin Goldberg, DHL; Foreword by Rabbi Naomi Levy*
Taps into timeless Jewish wisdom that teaches how to "hold on tightly" to the things that matter most while learning to "let go lightly" of the demands and worries that do not ultimately matter. 6 x 9, 192 pp, Quality PB, 978-1-58023-670-6 **$16.99**

The Bridge to Forgiveness: Stories and Prayers for Finding God and Restoring Wholeness *By Rabbi Karyn D. Kedar* 6 x 9, 176 pp, Quality PB, 978-1-58023-451-1 **$16.99**

The Empty Chair: Finding Hope and Joy—Timeless Wisdom from a Hasidic Master, Rebbe Nachman of Breslov *Adapted by Moshe Mykoff and the Breslov Research Institute*
4 x 6, 128 pp, Deluxe PB w/ flaps, 978-1-879045-67-5 **$9.99**

A Formula for Proper Living: Practical Lessons from Life and Torah *By Rabbi Abraham J. Twerski, MD* 6 x 9, 144 pp, HC, 978-1-58023-402-3 **$19.99**

The Gentle Weapon: Prayers for Everyday and Not-So-Everyday Moments—Timeless Wisdom from the Teachings of the Hasidic Master, Rebbe Nachman of Breslov *Adapted by Moshe Mykoff and S. C. Mizrahi, together with the Breslov Research Institute*
4 x 6, 144 pp, Deluxe PB w/ flaps, 978-1-58023-022-3 **$9.99**

The God Upgrade: Finding Your 21st-Century Spirituality in Judaism's 5,000-Year-Old Tradition *By Rabbi Jamie Korngold; Foreword by Rabbi Harold M. Schulweis*
6 x 9, 176 pp, Quality PB, 978-1-58023-443-6 **$15.99**

God Whispers: Stories of the Soul, Lessons of the Heart *By Rabbi Karyn D. Kedar*
6 x 9, 176 pp, Quality PB, 978-1-58023-088-9 **$16.99**

God's To-Do List: 103 Ways to Be an Angel and Do God's Work on Earth *By Dr. Ron Wolfson* 6 x 9, 144 pp, Quality PB, 978-1-58023-301-9 **$16.99**

Happiness and the Human Spirit: The Spirituality of Becoming the Best You Can Be *By Rabbi Abraham J. Twerski, MD*
6 x 9, 176 pp, Quality PB, 978-1-58023-404-7 **$16.99**; HC, 978-1-58023-343-9 **$19.99**

Life's Daily Blessings: Inspiring Reflections on Gratitude and Joy for Every Day, Based on Jewish Wisdom *By Rabbi Kerry M. Olitzky* 4½ x 6½, 368 pp, Quality PB, 978-1-58023-396-5 **$16.99**

The Magic of Hebrew Chant: Healing the Spirit, Transforming the Mind, Deepening Love *By Rabbi Shefa Gold; Foreword by Sylvia Boorstein*
6 x 9, 352 pp, Quality PB, 978-1-58023-671-3 **$24.99**

Restful Reflections: Nighttime Inspiration to Calm the Soul, Based on Jewish Wisdom *By Rabbi Kerry M. Olitzky and Rabbi Lori Forman-Jacobi* 4½ x 6½, 448 pp, Quality PB, 978-1-58023-091-9 **$16.99**

Sacred Intentions: Morning Inspiration to Strengthen the Spirit, Based on Jewish Wisdom *By Rabbi Kerry M. Olitzky and Rabbi Lori Forman-Jacobi* 4½ x 6½, 448 pp, Quality PB, 978-1-58023-061-2 **$16.99**

The Seven Questions You're Asked in Heaven: Reviewing and Renewing Your Life on Earth *By Dr. Ron Wolfson* 6 x 9, 176 pp, Quality PB, 978-1-58023-407-8 **$16.99**

Kabbalah / Mysticism

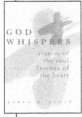

Ehyeh: A Kabbalah for Tomorrow
By Rabbi Arthur Green, PhD 6 x 9, 224 pp, Quality PB, 978-1-58023-213-5 **$18.99**

The Gift of Kabbalah: Discovering the Secrets of Heaven, Renewing Your Life on Earth
By Tamar Frankiel, PhD 6 x 9, 256 pp, Quality PB, 978-1-58023-141-1 **$18.99**

Jewish Mysticism and the Spiritual Life: Classical Texts, Contemporary Reflections *Edited by Dr. Lawrence Fine, Dr. Eitan Fishbane and Rabbi Or N. Rose*
6 x 9, 256 pp, HC, 978-1-58023-434-4 **$24.99**; Quality PB, 978-1-58023-719-2 **$18.99**

Seek My Face: A Jewish Mystical Theology *By Rabbi Arthur Green, PhD*
6 x 9, 304 pp, Quality PB, 978-1-58023-130-5 **$19.95**

Zohar: Annotated & Explained Translation & Annotation by Dr. Daniel C. Matt; Foreword by Andrew Harvey 5½ x 8½, 176 pp, Quality PB, 978-1-893361-51-5 **$18.99**
(A book from SkyLight Paths, Jewish Lights' sister imprint)

See also *The Way Into Jewish Mystical Tradition* in The Way Into... Series.

Spirituality

Amazing Chesed: Living a Grace-Filled Judaism
By Rabbi Rami Shapiro Drawing from ancient and contemporary, traditional and
non-traditional Jewish wisdom, reclaims the idea of grace in Judaism.
6 x 9, 176 pp, Quality PB, 978-1-58023-624-9 **$16.99**

Jewish with Feeling: A Guide to Meaningful Jewish Practice
By Rabbi Zalman Schachter-Shalomi with Joel Segel
Takes off from basic questions like "Why be Jewish?" and whether the word God
still speaks to us today and lays out a vision for a whole-person Judaism.
5½ x 8½, 288 pp, Quality PB, 978-1-58023-691-1 **$19.99**

Perennial Wisdom for the Spiritually Independent: Sacred Teachings—
Annotated & Explained *Annotation by Rami Shapiro; Foreword by Richard Rohr*
Weaves sacred texts and teachings from the world's major religions into a coherent exploration of the five core questions at the heart of every religion's search.
5½ x 8½, 336 pp, Quality PB Original, 978-1-59473-515-8 **$16.99**

Aleph-Bet Yoga: Embodying the Hebrew Letters for Physical and Spiritual Well-Being
By Steven A. Rapp; Foreword by Tamar Frankiel, PhD, and Judy Greenfeld; Preface by Hart Lazer
7 x 10, 128 pp, b/w photos, Quality PB, Lay-flat binding, 978-1-58023-162-6 **$16.95**

A Book of Life: Embracing Judaism as a Spiritual Practice
By Rabbi Michael Strassfeld 6 x 9, 544 pp, Quality PB, 978-1-58023-247-0 **$24.99**

Bringing the Psalms to Life: How to Understand and Use the Book of Psalms
By Rabbi Daniel F. Polish, PhD 6 x 9, 208 pp, Quality PB, 978-1-58023-157-2 **$18.99**

Does the Soul Survive? A Jewish Journey to Belief in Afterlife, Past Lives &
Living with Purpose *By Rabbi Elie Kaplan Spitz; Foreword by Brian L. Weiss, MD*
6 x 9, 288 pp, Quality PB, 978-1-58023-165-7 **$18.99**

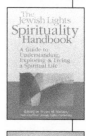

Entering the Temple of Dreams: Jewish Prayers, Movements and Meditations for
the End of the Day *By Tamar Frankiel, PhD, and Judy Greenfeld*
7 x 10, 192 pp, illus., Quality PB, 978-1-58023-079-7 **$16.95**

First Steps to a New Jewish Spirit: Reb Zalman's Guide to Recapturing the
Intimacy & Ecstasy in Your Relationship with God *By Rabbi Zalman M. Schachter-Shalomi
with Donald Gropman* 6 x 9, 144 pp, Quality PB, 978-1-58023-182-4 **$16.95**

Foundations of Sephardic Spirituality: The Inner Life of Jews of the Ottoman Empire
By Rabbi Marc D. Angel, PhD 6 x 9, 224 pp, Quality PB, 978-1-58023-341-5 **$18.99**

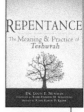

God & the Big Bang: Discovering Harmony between Science & Spirituality
By Dr. Daniel C. Matt 6 x 9, 216 pp, Quality PB, 978-1-879045-89-7 **$18.99**

God in Our Relationships: Spirituality between People from the Teachings of
Martin Buber *By Rabbi Dennis S. Ross* 5½ x 8½, 160 pp, Quality PB, 978-1-58023-147-3 **$16.95**

The Jewish Lights Spirituality Handbook: A Guide to Understanding, Exploring &
Living a Spiritual Life *Edited by Stuart M. Matlins*
6 x 9, 456 pp, Quality PB, 978-1-58023-093-3 **$19.99**

Judaism, Physics and God: Searching for Sacred Metaphors in a Post-Einstein World
By Rabbi David W. Nelson 6 x 9, 352 pp, Quality PB, inc. reader's discussion guide,
978-1-58023-306-4 **$18.99**; HC, 352 pp, 978-1-58023-252-4 **$24.99**

Meaning & Mitzvah: Daily Practices for Reclaiming Judaism through Prayer, God,
Torah, Hebrew, Mitzvot and Peoplehood *By Rabbi Goldie Milgram*
7 x 9, 336 pp, Quality PB, 978-1-58023-256-2 **$19.99**

Repentance: The Meaning and Practice of Teshuvah
By Dr. Louis E. Newman; Foreword by Rabbi Harold M. Schulweis; Preface by Rabbi Karyn D. Kedar
6 x 9, 256 pp, HC, 978-1-58023-426-9 **$24.99** Quality PB, 978-1-58023-718-5 **$18.99**

The Sabbath Soul: Mystical Reflections on the Transformative Power of Holy Time
Selection, Translation and Commentary by Eitan Fishbane, PhD
6 x 9, 208 pp, Quality PB, 978-1-58023-459-7 **$18.99**

Tanya, the Masterpiece of Hasidic Wisdom: Selections Annotated & Explained
Translation & Annotation by Rabbi Rami Shapiro; Foreword by Rabbi Zalman M. Schachter-Shalomi
5½ x 8½, 240 pp, Quality PB, 978-1-59473-275-1 **$18.99**

These Are the Words, 2nd Edition: A Vocabulary of Jewish Spiritual Life
By Rabbi Arthur Green, PhD 6 x 9, 320 pp, Quality PB, 978-1-58023-494-8 **$19.99**

About Jewish Lights

People of all faiths and backgrounds yearn for books that attract, engage, educate, and spiritually inspire.

Our principal goal is to stimulate thought and help all people learn about who the Jewish People are, where they come from, and what the future can be made to hold. While people of our diverse Jewish heritage are the primary audience, our books speak to people in the Christian world as well and will broaden their understanding of Judaism and the roots of their own faith.

We bring to you authors who are at the forefront of spiritual thought and experience. While each has something different to say, they all say it in a voice that you can hear.

Our books are designed to welcome you and then to engage, stimulate, and inspire. We judge our success not only by whether or not our books are beautiful and commercially successful, but by whether or not they make a difference in your life.

For your information and convenience, at the back of this book we have provided a list of other Jewish Lights books you might find interesting and useful. They cover all the categories of your life:

Bar/Bat Mitzvah	Life Cycle
Bible Study / Midrash	Meditation
Children's Books	Men's Interest
Congregation Resources	Parenting
Current Events / History	Prayer / Ritual / Sacred Practice
Ecology / Environment	Social Justice
Fiction: Mystery, Science Fiction	Spirituality
Grief / Healing	Theology / Philosophy
Holidays / Holy Days	Travel
Inspiration	Twelve Steps
Kabbalah / Mysticism / Enneagram	Women's Interest

Stuart M. Matlins, Publisher

Or phone, fax, mail or email to: **JEWISH LIGHTS Publishing**
Sunset Farm Offices, Route 4 • P.O. Box 237 • Woodstock, Vermont 05091
Tel: (802) 457-4000 • Fax: (802) 457-4004 • www.jewishlights.com
Credit card orders: **(800) 962-4544** (8:30AM–5:30PM EST Monday–Friday)
Generous discounts on quantity orders. SATISFACTION GUARANTEED. Prices subject to change.

CPSIA information can be obtained
at www.ICGtesting.com
Printed in the USA
BVHW03s2228200818
525147BV00001B/26/P